THE
VERIDICAN GOSPEL
OF
JESUS CHRIST

MMV

EDWARD J. GORDON

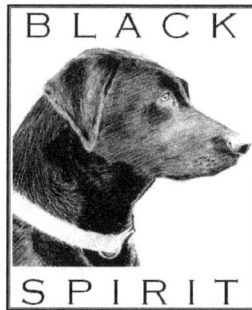

BLACK
SPIRIT

Originally published in the United Sates by:

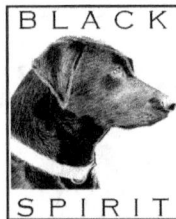

Black Spirit Publishing
P.O. Box 2428
PMB# 8443
Pensacola, FL 32513

ISBN 978-0-9838971-3-2

For rights information, contact Black Spirit Publishing
by mail or e-mail:

information@veridican.net

6 7 8 9 10

This Gospel harmony is dedicated to all who appreciate the life and teachings of Jesus Christ.

PREFACE

The Veridican Gospel of Jesus Christ is not a new Gospel. It's the same Gospel story that has existed for two thousand years. It's the same Gospel that's found in Matthew, Mark, Luke, or John. It's the same Gospel message from God to mankind that will never disappear. What makes the *Veridican Gospel* different is not the message it contains but how it conveys that message: the *Veridican Gospel of Jesus Christ* is a modern Gospel harmony.

A Gospel harmony is an attempt to unite the four Gospels of the New Testament into a single narrative. The earliest known Gospel harmony is the *Diatessaron* written by the 2nd century Christian apologist, Tatian. Tatian (120-185 A.D.) was a student of Justin Martyr in Rome but later became the leader of an Assyrian Christian sect known as the Encratites.

His *Diatessaron* would go on to be the standard Gospel record for the Syriac-speaking churches until the 5th-century, after which the Roman Church embraced the four separate gospels in their canon of scripture. Thereafter, the *Diatessaron* fell into disuse, and in fact, came to be considered a heretical document.

However, variations based on the *Diatessaron* continued to appear even into the Middle Ages. In the 16th century, there was a decided increase in the writing and publishing of Gospel harmonies, but unlike the *Diatessaron*, those harmonies were written in a *parallel column structure* (or PCS).

A PCS Gospel harmony takes the four Gospels of the New Testament and compares the verses side-by-side in four columns trying to line them up in such a way that they all support one another—as if they were all telling one unified story. That is not, however, the same thing as creating a single Gospel record out of the four. In other words, a PCS Gospel harmony is not a *true* Gospel harmony—not like the *Diatessaron*.

That said, the problem with trying to create a true Gospel harmony (a single Gospel record out of the four) has always been that the Gospels really don't match up very well. Matthew and Luke, for instance, have a lot of information not contained in Mark or John such as the birth narrative and the genealogies—not to mention there are conflicting accounts of the miracles Jesus performed as well as conflicting accounts of the crucifixion and his resurrection.

Even so, the Christian Church maintains that that each of the four Gospels is a Divinely inspired document, and thus, separately or together, represent the inerrant word of God. The Church, therefore, maintains that there are no contradictions, and that the Gospel is a single story. PCS harmonies are, therefore, used to show how similar the separate Gospel accounts are to one another.

But in fact, the New Testament Gospels *do* contradict each other, and they *are not* telling the same story, and in my opinion, as one who wants to honestly follow the real Jesus Christ, that discordance needs to be corrected; it has always needed to be corrected—just as Tatian thought it needed to be corrected shortly after the four Gospels appeared on the scene.

And so, the *Veridican Gospel of Jesus Christ* sets out to do exactly that. In the spirit of the *Diatessaron*, The *Veridican Gospel* is a true Gospel harmony. But the VGJC is not without its own issues.

Authority and readership are the first two problems. Who has the authority to be the editor that cuts up and reassembles the Gospel records so they fit together? Does one need to be inspired by the Holy Spirit as we believe the first Gospel writers were? Does one need to be a prophet acting on direct instructions from God? I, as the author of this text, cannot answer those questions. I believe what I have created is correct and the way God intended me to edit it—but I can't say of myself that I was inspired by the Holy Spirit in each editorial decision I made, and I will never consider myself to be a prophet. I hope I was accurate, but my accuracy is ultimately something only you—the reader—can judge.

But what readers? That's the second problem. In creating a true Gospel harmony, I am unequivocally creating a heretical document, so Christians are not going to be inclined to read it. Those who are not Christians, or not religious, and might not care about any such heresy are not likely to be interested in a Gospel narrative about Jesus Christ. The only readers likely to ever read the *Veridican Gospel*, therefore, are those who choose to follow the life and teachings of Jesus Christ, yet place themselves outside the Christian Church, and those are rare individuals indeed.

The Gospel of Thomas is another complication: *The Gospel of Thomas* was first discovered at the beginning of the twentieth century in Oxyrhynchus, Egypt, and its complete form was rediscovered as part of the Nag Hammadi library in 1945. It clearly contains important Gospel information, and it's thought by some scholars that the only reason it wasn't included in the canon of the New Testament is because it wasn't known to exist, or they didn't have a copy of it at that time (around 300 A.D.).

Thomas contains 114 sayings of Jesus Christ, some of which are in none of the other Gospels. It is believed by some scholars that *Thomas* may be the closest thing to the original Gospel record (a hypothetical Gospel called the *Q* document) that has ever been discovered. Few read it without immediately recognizing its transformative power, and now that it has been discovered and translated from its original Greek, it makes the New Testament Gospel record seem incomplete without it.

I know that my reading of *Thomas* in the 1990's changed my understanding of Jesus Christ, and it became the catalyst of my motivation to write the *Veridican Gospel*. It seemed to me (and still does) that if *Thomas* was left out of the Bible, and clearly should not have been, then perhaps the Church got it wrong all those centuries ago. Perhaps all along they should have taken the four New Testament Gospels and the *Gospel of Thomas* and used their ecclesiastical authority to create a single Gospel record. But they did not; they will not today, and so I did in 2005.

What exists now is the same 2005 edition, and it is the final edition of the Veridican Gospel. Separate printings have replaced older printings since then, but any changes to the text have been merely grammatical corrections and an updated preface.

It is said that the Holy Spirit guided the early writers to record the Gospels without error, but it's also a fact that the identity of those writers is lost in history. No one knows their real names or where they came from. So, we can never know their actual motivations or qualifications for writing a story about Jesus Christ. We only know the *effect* of their writing. Perhaps then it is the same with the *Veridican Gospel of Jesus Christ*. As the writer of it, I am no one in particular, but if one reads it and has a revelation of Jesus Christ, then obviously it has accomplished its purpose.

Since I was very young, I've been drawn to the life and teachings of Jesus Christ, and I was astounded when I first read *The Gospel of Thomas*. *The Veridican Gospel of Jesus Christ* is an attempt to honor Jesus and the Gospel record of his life. To the extent I have been successful in that mission I must leave to the judgment of my readers.

~ Edward Gordon

We don't know who the Gospel writers were. The names, Matthew, Mark, Luke, and John have merely been ascribed to them, nor do we know who the Thomas of the Gospel of Thomas was. Who they are, and where they got their story is a complete mystery. What we do know is the effect the story has on us when we read it.

CHAPTER 1

1. Many have undertaken to write the Gospel of Jesus Christ, but all who succeed have done so by dictating what the Spirit of Truth has spoken to them, and all who hear the Gospel hear it only through the Spirit of Truth who communicates it.

2. This is the record of the life and teachings of our Lord and Savior, the Son of Man, the Son of God, Jesus Christ.

3. For the living Christ has shown us that whosoever discovers the truth of His secret sayings will never taste death, but will inherit eternal life.

4. In the beginning was the Word, and the Word was with God, and the Word was God. The universe has come into being from that Word, and all things are composed of it. The Word is life. And that life is the Light within us.

5. And though the Light shines in the darkness of the world, the world has not understood it; for the Light came into the world and took the form of a man, and though the Light was the Creator of the world, the world did not recognize Him.

6. But to those who do recognize Him, He has given the power to become one with Him who is one with God.

7. In the past, God gave us the law, but Jesus Christ has fulfilled the law with truth, love, and unity. So, we have passed through the law and into the grace of God.

8. For no one has ever seen God except those who are begotten of God. Jesus Christ—the Son of God—has shown God to us.

CHAPTER 2

1. In ancient times, during the reign of Augustus Caesar in Rome, and Herod Agrippa in Israel, there was a servant of God named John who preached in the wilderness saying, "Repent, for the kingdom of heaven is at hand!"

2. John wore only animal skins for clothing and ate only bugs and wild honey for food. He would baptize people in the river as a sign of their repentance from sin.

3. But when he saw the religious leaders coming to be baptized, he shouted at them saying, "You brood of lying evildoers! Who told you to flee from the coming wrath of God?

4. "Make straight your way to God, and repent from your sins! I baptize you with water, but one is coming whose shoes I am not worthy to carry.

5. "He will baptize with the Holy Spirit and with fire. Indeed, His winnowing fork is in His hand, and He will gather His wheat into the granary, but the chaff He will burn in an unquenchable fire.

6. "Do not say to yourself, 'I am a child of God—as if that can save you—for God could make a child from one of these stones if He wanted to."

7. And so with many exhortations, John the Baptist encouraged the people to live according to his teachings.

8. But one day, as he was baptizing, he saw Jesus in the crowd of people, and Jesus came to him.

9. John pointed at Jesus and shouted, "Behold, the Lamb of God who takes away the sins of the world!"

10. And John was in awe of Jesus and said to two of his disciples, "He was there all the time, and yet I did not see Him. He was all around me and existed before me, and yet I did not know Him.

11. "I baptize with plain water, but it is not enough. He has come into the world and all judgment is with Him. Indeed, the axe is at the root, and all the trees that do not bear fruit will be cut down and thrown into the fire."

12. Then Jesus came to John to be baptized, but John stopped Him saying: "I must be baptized by You, and yet You have come to me?"

13. But Jesus said to him: "Let it be this way for now; for it is fitting that we should fulfill all righteousness."

14. And John said, "For this purpose I came into the world, baptizing with water."

15. Then John baptized Jesus, and as Jesus arose from the water, John saw the spirit of God in the form of a dove de-

scend upon Him, and a voice from heaven said, "You are My Son in whom I am well pleased."

16. Immediately after this, Jesus left and went into the wilderness, and John watched Him leave, and said to his disciples, "This is the one who is greater than I. He must increase, and I must decrease."

17. Soon after this, Herod was bothered in his conscience by the things John was saying about his many evil deeds, so he added this one to them: He cast John into prison.

CHAPTER 3

1. In the wilderness, Jesus was lead by the Holy Spirit to be tempted by Satan.

2. He fasted for forty days, and at the end of it, He was hungry. Then Satan came to Him saying, "If you are the Son of God, why do You not tell these stones to become bread?"

3. But Jesus said to him, "One does not live on bread alone. One lives by every word that proceeds from the mouth of God."

4. Then Satan took Him to the Holy City, and they stood on the very pinnacle of the temple, and he said to Him, "Why do You not jump off from here? If You are the Son of God, He will command His angels to protect You and bear You up, even to keep You from striking Your foot against a stone."

5. But Jesus said to him, "You will not test God."

6. After that, Satan took Jesus to the top of a high mountain, and below them, all the kingdoms of the world shone in their glory, and Satan said to Him, "All of this is mine. It has been given to me, and I can give it to whomever I want. I will give it to You if You will only fall down and worship me."

7. But Jesus said to him, "I will serve My Father and He alone. Satan, be gone from me."

8. At that, Satan left Him for a more opportune time, and the angels of God ministered to the Son of Man.

CHAPTER 4

1. From the wilderness, Jesus returned to His hometown and began to preach a message of repentance from the world. In the temple, on the sabbath, He stood and quoted from the scriptures:

2. "The Spirit of the Lord is upon Me, for He has anointed Me to preach the Gospel to the poor. He has sent Me to announce the release of the captives, and to recover the sight of the blind. He has sent Me to free the oppressed and to proclaim the favorable year of the Lord."

3. At that, He closed the scriptures and handed it back to the priest and sat down, and the eyes of the entire congregation were fixed on Him. And He said to them, "Today, in your hearing, the scriptures are fulfilled."

4. And a rumble went through the crowed and they said among themselves, "Who is this? Is this not Jesus? Do we

not know His mother and sisters and brothers? Is He not merely the son of Joseph—a carpenter from Nazareth? How dare He preach to us!"

5. So He said to them, "No doubt you will tell Me to tend to Myself—'physician, heal thyself,' but I say to you, a prophet is never accepted in his hometown. The Son of Man has come and is rejected by those who knew Him before, even by the members of His own household."

6. All the people in the temple were filled with rage as they heard Him speak these words. "We are God's chosen people," they said. "Who are You to set Yourself above us?"

7. And they drove Him out of the Temple to the edge of the city near a high cliff in order to throw Him off and to kill Him.

8. But He walked through the midst of them and went on His way.

9. From the crowd, two men (John and Andrew) followed after Jesus, because they heard John the Baptist's testimony concerning Jesus, and they said to Him, "Teacher, where do You stay?"

10. And Jesus said to them, "Follow Me, and you will see where I am." So, they followed Him and stayed with Him, for the night was at hand.

11. In the morning, Andrew found his brother, Simon, and said to him, "We have found the Christ!" And when he brought him to Jesus, Jesus looked at Simon and said, "From now on you will be called Peter, and you will be the rock upon which My church is built."

12. Then Jesus set out on His way to find Philip, and when He had found him, He said to him, "Follow Me." And Philip instantly recognized Christ as all that the law and prophets had spoken of. So Philip went out and found Nathaniel.

13. But when Nathaniel heard of Jesus from Philip, he said, "How could any good come from Nazareth?"

14. "Come and see," Philip said. And when Jesus saw Nathaniel He declared, "Here is a true child of God in whom there is no deceit!"

15. "How do you know me?" Nathaniel asked. And Jesus revealed to him, "Before Philip called you, I saw you when you were alone under the fig tree." Then Nathaniel recognized Jesus as the Christ and said, "My Teacher, You are the Son of God. You are the King of heaven!"

16. Then Jesus asked him, "Do you believe only because I said I saw you when you were alone? You will have more than this. For you will see angels descending on and ascending from the Son of Man."

17. Later, while standing on the edge of a lake, a crowd had gathered to hear Him speak the words of God, and as they pressed toward Him, He saw two fishing boats sitting on the shore of the lake.

18. He got into one of the boats, which belonged to Peter, and asked him to push off slightly from the shore. There He sat in the boat and taught the people.

19. And when He had finished speaking, He turned to Peter and said, "Take us out into deep water and let down your nets for a new catch."

20. Peter answered and said, "Lord, we have worked all night and caught nothing, but I will do as You say."

21. As soon as the nets were in deep water, they began to fill with fish, to the point where they were starting to break. And as they hauled in the nets, they were so full that the boat was beginning to sink. Therefore, James, who was with them, called to other boats to come and take some of the fish.

22. And when they were back on shore, and the awesome power of Christ was revealed to Peter by this miracle, Peter fell at the feet of Jesus and said, "Go away from me Lord! Do You not realize I am a sinful man!"

23. But Jesus lifted Peter up and said to him, "Follow Me, and I will make you a fisher of souls."

24. So, Peter left behind everything and followed Jesus.

25. As Jesus traveled with His disciples, they entered a village; and Martha, a woman known to Thaddeus, welcomed them into her home.

26. Martha had a sister called Mary, who sat at the Lord's feet, listening to His words.

27. But Martha was distracted with all her preparations; and she came to Jesus and said, "Lord, do You not care that my sister has left me to do all the serving alone? Why do You not tell her to get up and help me?"

28. But the Lord answered and said to her, "Martha, Martha, you are worried and bothered about so many things; but only one thing is necessary, and Mary has chosen that good work. It shall not be taken from her."

29. And from that point forward, Mary became a disciple of Christ, following Him and growing into the image of her Lord.

30. When Jesus had gathered His disciples and they had set out on their way, Mary asked Him, "What are your disciples like?"

31. And He said to her, "They are like little children living in a field that is not their own. When the owners of the land return, they say, 'Give our land back to us.' So, the children give back everything, even the clothes they are wearing, and they return the field to its rightful owners—and the children go home."

CHAPTER 5

1. A few days later, Jesus and His disciples were invited to a wedding. When the wine for the wedding ran out, the mother of Jesus said to Him, "The wine is gone, and the guests are left without any."

2. But Jesus said to her, "Woman, what has that to do with us? My hour has not yet come?"

3. But His mother said to the servants, "Whatever He tells you to do, do it."

4. So Jesus went to the thirty-gallon water pots used for ceremonial purification and found them empty. He told the servants to fill them to the top with water. And when they had done so, Jesus told the servants, "Take a cup of this to the master of the ceremony."

5. When the servant took the cup to the master of the ceremony, he sampled the water, which had now become wine, and

said to the bridegroom, "Everyone else brings out good wine, and when it is exhausted and everyone is drunk, they bring out the bad wine; but now I see that You have saved the best for last."

6. This sign Jesus gave to His disciples, and it manifested His glory to them, and they believed in Him.

7. From there, Jesus took His disciples to the top of a mountain to avoid the crowds of people who had heard of the miracle of the wine.

8. When they arrived at the top, they sat around Him, and He taught them saying:

9. "Blessed are the poor in Spirit, for it is they who find the kingdom of heaven.

10. "Blessed are you who are alone and chosen, for you will find the kingdom you came from and you will return to it.

11. "Blessed are the ones who toil in the Spirit, for they will gain eternal life.

12. "Blessed are those who count the world as loss, for they will return to glory.

13. "Blessed are those who endure the injuries of this generation without resentment, for they will own the entire creation.

14. "Blessed are those who hunger and thirst for righteousness, for in Me they shall be satisfied.

15. "Blessed are the merciful, for they will find mercy.

16. "Blessed are the pure in Spirit, for they shall see God.

17. "Blessed are those who are persecuted in their hearts, for they will find the Father.

18. "Blessed are you when people insult you and persecute you, and lie about you on account of Me. Rejoice in this and be glad, for so their fathers treated all the prophets and saints who came before you.

19. "But woe unto those who are rich in this world, for their reward is the world.

20. "Woe to those who are self-righteous and judge themselves to be good, for their wretchedness will keep them far from the kingdom.

21. "Woe to those who love their life in this world, for their loss will be complete.

22. "And woe to those who are well praised in this world, for so it is the world that praises all manner of evil."

CHAPTER 6

1. Jesus said, "You are the salt of the earth, but if the salt looses its saltiness, what good is it? How can it ever be made salty again? It is good for nothing, except to be thrown down and trampled on. Therefore, remain in Me.

2. "There is light within a person of light, and that light shines on the whole world. If it does not shine, the world is dark.

3. "You are the light of the world. A city at night on a hill cannot be hidden, and a lamp is not put under a basket, but rather it is set up high so that it gives light to all who are near it.

4. "Therefore, let your light so shine before all that they may see your good works and give glory to your Father in heaven.

5. "Do not think that I have come to destroy the law. I did not come to destroy it but to fulfill it.

6. "For truly, I tell you, until heaven and earth pass away, nothing shall be taken away from the law until all of it is fulfilled.

7. "And until your righteousness surpasses that of the religious leaders, you can never enter the kingdom of heaven. Therefore, remain in Me.

8. "Love one another as I have loved you. Love your neighbor as yourself.

9. "Do unto others as you would have it done unto you.

10. "But do not love only your friends; even the evildoers love their friends. Love your enemies, as well.

11. "If you only love those who love you in return what reward is that? Even the sinners return love for love. If you greet only those in your inner circle, how is that any different than a commoner? Instead, you must be greater.

12. "Do good to those who hate you, and pray for those who hurt you.

13. "Do not resist an evil person, but if someone slaps you on one cheek, turn the other to them as well.

14. "And if someone steals your coat, give them your shirt as well.

15. "Bless those who curse you, and if someone forces you to walk one mile with them, walk two instead.

16. "If someone wants to borrow from you, or asks something of you, give to them freely and do not expect them to return it.

17. "In these acts, you will find that God is in you, for He cannot be offended, and He cares for the ungrateful and evildoers. He sends rain to the just and the unjust.

18. "Therefore, be merciful, even as God is merciful. Be perfect, even as God is perfect.

19. "You have heard it said, 'Do not murder,' but I say to you that anyone who is angry with another is guilty of murder. Anyone who says to their neighbor, 'You fool!' is in danger of the fires of hell.

20. "Therefore, if you are praying to God and remember that your neighbor has something against you, stop praying and go be reconciled to your neighbor, and then return to prayer.

21. "If your brother or sister sins against you, rebuke them. But if they come to you and repent forgive them. If they sin against you seven times a day and seven times a day come to you and say 'I repent,' forgive them seven times a day.

22. "You have heard it said, 'Do not commit adultery,' but I tell you that any person who looks upon another with lust has already committed adultery in their heart.

23. "Therefore, if your right eye makes you sin, pluck it out and throw it away. It is better to enter the kingdom of heaven with one eye, than to end up in hell with two.

24. "If your right hand causes you to sin, cut it off. It is better to end up in the kingdom of heaven with one hand than to end up in hell with two.

25. "Do not judge others, and you will not be judged. Do not condemn others, and you will not be condemned. Pardon others, and you will be pardoned.

26. "Whenever you stand in prayer, forgive—if you have anything against anyone—so that your Father in heaven will also forgive your transgressions.

27. "For in the way that you judge others, you will be judged. How can you say to your neighbor, 'Neighbor, let me remove the speck from your eye,' when you have a beam in your own eye?

28. "And if a beam remains in your eye, then you are blind and you are leading the blind until you both fall into a pit.

29. "You hypocrite! First, remove the beam from your own eye, and then you will see clearly to remove the speck from your neighbor's eye.

30. "Behold, a good tree produces good fruit, a bad tree, bad fruit. One does not find grapes among thorns. Instead, a good person produces good from the good treasure within their heart; likewise, a bad person produces only evil from the evil within them.

31. "Therefore, do not cast your pearls before swine, for they will only trample them. And why give to dogs that which is holy? They will only turn and attack you."

CHAPTER 7

1. "Beware of practicing your righteousness before others, so that you will be noticed. If you are righteous for the notice of others, then your reward is from others, and you will have no reward from your Father in heaven.

2. "So, when you give to the poor, do not publicize it as the hypocrites do so they will receive the honor of people; for I tell you in truth, they have their full reward.

3. "But when you give to the poor, do not let your left hand know what your right hand is doing. Then your giving which is done in secret will be seen by your Father who sees all things kept in secret, and your reward will be with Him.

4. "When you pray, you are not to be like the hypocrites. For they love to pray in public where people see them. In truth, I tell you, the notice of others is their only reward.

5. "But when you pray, go into your inner room, close the door, and pray to your Father who is in there with you, and your Father who sees what is done in secret places will reward you.

6. "And when you pray, do not use vain repetitions like the heathens use. For they think they will be heard through their repetitions and many words. But your Father knows what you need, even before you ask for it.

7. "Therefore, when you pray, do so in this manner:

8. 'Our Father who is in heaven, hallowed be Your name. Your kingdom come, Your will be done on Earth as it is in heaven. Give us this day, our daily bread, and forgive our trespasses as we forgive those who trespass against us. And lead us not into temptation, but deliver us from evil; for Yours is the kingdom, the power, and the glory for ever and ever. Amen.'

9. "For the one who has ears to hear, hear this: if you forgive others, you will be forgiven. If you will not forgive, you stand unforgiven.

10. "When you fast, do not put on a gloomy face as the hypocrites do, for they love to show their sufferings to find favor among the people—truly they have their reward.

11. "But when you fast, keep up your appearance, and do not let your suffering show, then your Father who is in secret, and sees all things in secret, will reward you.

12. "And do not store up riches on this earth where moths and rust destroy them, and thieves break in to steal them. Rather, store up treasures in heaven that endure and fail not, where nothing can destroy them and no one can ever take them away.

13. "For wherever your treasure is stored, there also is your heart.

14. "For this reason, I tell you, do not worry about your life, regarding what you will eat or drink. Do not worry about your body regarding what clothes you will wear. Is life not more than food? Is it not more than clothes?

15. "Look at your Father's world: Do the birds of the air plant and harvest, and store up in barns for the future? No. Yet your Father takes care of them their entire lives. Are not you worth more than a bird?

16. "And why worry about clothing? Look at your Father's world; does not everything have the clothes it needs? See how even the flowers are adorned? And yet they do not toil or spin wool, and yet they are taken care of. Not even kings are dressed so finely.

17. "Are you not worth more than a flower that is alive today, and tomorrow is plucked up and thrown into the fire?

18. "And who of you by worrying can add a single hour to their life?

19. "Oh, you of little faith! Do not chase after what you will eat or what you will wear—let the world follow these things. Your Father already knows you need them.

20. "But seek first the kingdom of God and the righteousness that comes from dwelling therein, and all these things will be added unto you."

21. "The eye is the lamp of the body. If your vision is clear, your whole mind will be clear, but if your sight is dim, your whole mind will be full of darkness. If the only light you have is darkness, how great is that darkness?"

22. Then His disciples asked Him, "Where is the kingdom of God that we might find it?"

23. And He said to them, "Those who seek the kingdom should not stop until they find it. When they find it, they will be disturbed by what they find, but that will turn to marvel, and when they marvel, they will reign over all things.

24. "When you make the two into one, and when you make the inner like the outer, and the outer like the inner, and when you make the upper like the lower, and the male and female into a single one, so that the male will not be male nor the female a female. When you make eyes in place of an eye, a hand in place of a hand, a foot in place of a foot, an image in place of an image, then you will enter the kingdom of God.

25. "If your leaders say to you, 'Look, the kingdom is in the sky, then the birds will make it in before you do, or if they say it is in the sea, then the fish will precede you. Rather, the kingdom of God is within you.

26. "Suppose one of you has a friend, and you go to that friend at midnight and say to him, 'Friend, lend me some food from your stores, because a companion of mine has come to me from a journey, and I have nothing to set before him.'

27. "And from inside, the friend answers and says, 'Do not bother me. The door is locked for the night, and the children and I are in bed. I cannot get up now and give you anything.'

28. "I say to you, even though she will not get up and give him anything just because he is a friend, she will get up and give him something if he persists in asking her.

29. "So then ask, and it will be given to you. Seek, and you will find. Knock and the door will be opened to you. For everyone who asks, receives; and everyone who seeks, finds; and to everyone who knocks, the door is opened.

30. "Or who among you when your child asks for a loaf of bread will give her a stone, or if she asks for fish will give her a snake?

31. If you being evil will give good gifts to your children, how much more will your Father in heaven give the kingdom to those who ask Him?

32. "But the gate to the kingdom is narrow, and few are those who ever enter it. Wide is the gate that leads to destruction, and many are they who pass through it.

33. "Strive, therefore, to enter through the narrow gate, for many will try to enter the kingdom of God, but will be unable to.

34. "Beware of the false teachers who come in my name. They are like wolves in sheep's clothing. You will know them by the fruit they bear; for grapes are not gathered from thorns nor are figs gathered from thistles.

35. "Every good tree bears good fruit, but the bad bears bad fruit. A good tree cannot produce bad fruit, and a bad tree cannot produce good fruit.

36. "All trees that do not produce good fruit are cut down and thrown into the fire.

37. "Know that not everyone who says to me, 'Lord, Lord,' will enter the kingdom of heaven, but the one who does the will of our Father in heaven will enter—for that is the good fruit.

38. "Many will say to Me on their last day, when they see the Son of Man in His glory, 'Lord, Lord, did we not prophesy in Your name, and in Your name cast out demons, and in Your name perform many miracles?'

39. "And then I will say to them, 'I never knew you. Depart from Me, you workers of iniquity, to the place prepared for the devil and his angels.'

40. "So why do you call Me, 'Lord, Lord' and do not do what I say?

41. "Yet everyone who hears these words of Mine and puts them into practice may be compared to a wise person who built their house on a rock. When the rain came, and the winds blew, and the floodwaters rose, the house did not fall, for it was founded on the rock.

42. "And everyone who hears these words of Mine and does not put them into practice will be like a foolish person who built their house on the sand. When the rain came, and the winds blew, and the floodwaters rose, the house fell, for it had a weak foundation—and great was the fall of it."

CHAPTER 8

1. After He had taught His disciples, they left together and went into the town, and there He entered the temple and began to teach.

2. All were amazed at his teachings, for He taught them as one who had authority and not as the legalists do.

3. Just then a man in the Church with an unclean spirit cried out to Jesus, "What business do we have with each other? Have You come to destroy us? I know who You are; You are the Holy One of God!"

4. But Jesus rebuked the spirit, saying, "Be silent and come out of him." And throwing the man into convulsions and with a loud cry, the spirit came out of him.

5. All who witnessed the event were amazed and debated among themselves, saying, "What is this? A new teaching with authority so that even the unclean spirits obey Him?"

6. And thereafter the news about Jesus spread throughout the land.

7. After this, they came out of the temple and went to the house of Peter and Andrew, along with James. Peter's mother was lying sick with fever, so they spoke to Jesus about her.

8. And He came to her and raised her up, taking her by the hand, and the fever left her, and she served them and the entire house.

9. After the sun had set, and darkness fell upon the land, they began bringing Him all who were ill and those who were demon possessed. And the whole city had gathered at the door.

10. He healed many who were ill with different diseases and cast out many demons, and He did not permit the demons to speak, because they knew who He was.

11. For it was being said of Him, "He has taken away our infirmities and carried away our disease."

12. In the early morning, while it was still dark, Jesus arose, left the house and went away to a secluded place in the countryside and was praying there.

13. Peter and his companions searched for Him, and when they found Him, they said to Him, "Everyone is looking for You."

14. And Jesus said, "I took my stand in the midst of the world, and in the flesh I appeared to them. I found them all drunk, and I did not find any of them thirsty. My soul aches for the children of humanity, for they are blind in their hearts and

do not see. They have come into the world empty, and they seek to depart from the world empty."

15. "But what of us?" Peter asked.

16. Jesus answered saying, "If they ask you where you came from, say to them, 'We have come from the Light, from the place where the Light came into being by Itself, established Itself, and appeared in our image.'

17. "If they ask you for proof of the Father in you, say to them, 'It is motion and rest.'"

18. Then Jesus said, "Let us go somewhere else to the towns nearby, so that I may preach there also; for this is what I came for."

19. And He went into the Church preaching and casting out demons, and a leper came to Him, beseeching Him, and falling to his knees before Him, saying, "If You are willing, You can make me clean."

20. With compassion, Jesus stretched out His hand and touched him, saying, "I am willing; be clean."

21. Immediately the man's leprosy was cleansed.

22. And Jesus said to him, "See that you tell no one, but rather go and show yourself to the Pharisees and religious leaders and live among them as a clean man."

23. Now, when Jesus had returned to His hometown, several days later, it was heard that He was at home.

24. At that time, many gathered around His home, so that there was no longer any room, not even near the door, and He spoke to them.

25. But four men came bringing to Him a paralytic, but being unable to get to Him because of the crowd, they cut a hole in the roof above Him, and when they had done so, they lowered the stretcher on which the paralytic lay until he was in front of Jesus.

26. And Jesus, seeing their faith, said to the man on the stretcher, "Son, your sins are forgiven you."

27. But some of the religious leaders were sitting there and reasoning in their hearts, "Why does this man speak like that? He is blaspheming against God. Who can forgive sins but God alone?"

28. And Jesus was aware in His spirit what they were reasoning in their hearts and said to them, "Which is easier, to say to the paralyzed man, 'Get up and walk,' or to say to him, 'Your sins are forgiven'?

29. "But so you will know that the Son of Man has authority on earth to forgive sins…" He turned to the paralytic and said, "Get up. Pick up your stretcher and go home."

30. And he immediately picked up his stretcher and went out in front of everyone. And all were amazed and glorified God saying, "We have never seen this sort of thing before. Who knew that God had given such authority to men?"

31. Then Jesus left and went out by the seashore and all the people were coming to Him, and He taught them.

CHAPTER 9

1. Now, there was a religious leader named Nicodemus who
    came to Jesus in the night and said to Him, "Teacher, we
    know that You are sent from God to instruct us, for no one
    can give the signs that you give unless God is with Him. But
    You say You have a kingdom; where is that kingdom?"

2. Jesus answered him saying, "Truly I tell you, unless you are
    born again, you cannot see the kingdom of God."

3. Nicodemus asked, "How can I be born again when I am old?
    I cannot re-enter my mother's womb and be born a second
    time."

4. But Jesus said, "Unless you are born of water and of the
    spirit, you cannot enter the kingdom of God. That which is
    born of flesh is flesh; that which is born of spirit is spirit.

5. "If flesh came into being because of spirit, that is a marvel,
    but if spirit came into being because of the body—that is a
    marvel of marvels. And yet you marvel not at how such
    great wealth has come to dwell in this poverty.

6. "Do not be amazed that I said, 'You must be born again.' The wind blows where it will and you hear the sound of it, but you cannot tell where it came from or where it is going; so it is with everyone born of the spirit."

7. Nicodemus said to Him, "But how is that possible?"

8. And Jesus said to him, "You are a teacher of Israel, and yet you do not know these things?

9. "Truly, we speak of what we know and testify to that which we have seen, but you do not accept our testimony. If I told you earthly things and you do not believe, how can you believe if I tell you about heavenly things?

10. "No one has ever ascended into heaven that did not come from heaven.

11. "But the Son of Man must be lifted up, and all those who look upon Him and believe in Him will have eternal life.

12. "For God so loved the world that He gave His only begotten Son, that whosoever believes in Him shall not perish, but have everlasting life.

13. "For God did not send the Son into the world to condemn the world, but rather to save the world through Him.

14. "The person who believes in the Son is not judged, but the one who does not believe stands judged already by the very fact that they do not believe.

15. "And this then is the judgment: The Light has come into the world, but the world loves darkness because the deeds of people are evil.

16. "And so I tell you, whoever has come to know the world has discovered a carcass, and whosoever discovers that carcass, of that person the world is not worthy.

17. "For everyone who does evil hates the Light and will not come into it for fear that their deeds will be exposed.

18. "But those who practice truth come into the Light so that it may be seen that the works they do originate in God.

19. "I am the Light that is over all things. I am all; from Me all came forth and to Me all is attained. Split a piece of wood, and I am there. Lift up a stone, and you will find Me there."

20. The next day, Jesus went out and noticed a tax collector named Matthew sitting in his tax booth, and He said to him, "Follow Me."

21. And Matthew left everything and followed Him.

22. That evening, Matthew held a large dinner at his home. There was a great crowd of tax collectors and other people who were sitting at the table with them.

23. The Pharisees and the scribes began complaining to His disciples saying, "Why does He eat and drink with tax collectors and common sinners?"

24. But Jesus answered and said to them, "It is not the healthy who need a physician but rather it is the sick. I have not come to call the righteous to repentance; I have come to call the sinners. But go and learn what God means when He says, 'I desire mercy and not sacrifice.'"

25. So they said to Him, "The disciples of John the Baptist often fast and offer prayers at this time, and so do the religious leaders, but Yours are eating and drinking."

26. And Jesus said to them, "You cannot make the friends of the bridegroom fast while the bridegroom is with them. But the days will come when the bridegroom is taken away from them, and in those days they will fast.

27. "For truly I tell you, if you do not fast from the world, you will never find the Father's kingdom."

28. Then He told a parable: "No one makes a patch from unshrunk cloth and puts it on an old garment. If they do, the patch will shrink and tear the garment and the hole will be bigger than before the patch.

29. "And no one takes new wine and puts it in old wineskins. If they do, the old wineskins will burst and the wine will be spilled out and the skins ruined. Rather, new wine is put into new wineskins and both are preserved.

30. "And no one after drinking the old wine wishes for new wine. For they reason with themselves that the old wine is good enough."

CHAPTER 10

1. The next day, Jesus was sitting by a well, for He was weary from walking.

2. There came a woman to the well to draw water, and Jesus said to her, "Will you give Me something to drink?" For His disciples had gone away into the city to buy food.

3. The woman said to Him, "How is it that You, a Jew, ask a drink of me, a woman of Samaria?" For Jews have no dealings with Samaritans.

4. Jesus said to her, "If you knew the gift of God and who it is that says to you, 'Will you give Me a drink?' you would have asked Him, and He would have given you living water."

5. "Sir," the woman said, "You have nothing to draw water from the well and it is too deep. Where then do You get living water? You are not greater than our forefathers are You, who gave us this well and drank from it themselves?"

6. Jesus answered and said, "Whoever drinks from this well will get thirsty soon after, but whoever drinks the water I give will never thirst; but the water that I give will become in them a well of water springing up to eternal life."

7. The woman said to Him, "Sir, give me this water, so I will no longer thirst nor have to come all the way to this well to draw water from it."

8. Jesus said to her, "Go, call to your husband and come back here."

9. The woman answered and said, "I have no husband."

10. Jesus said to her, "You have said in truth that you have no husband, for you have had five husbands and the one you are currently with is not your husband."

11. The woman replied, "I can tell that You are a prophet, so tell me what is true: Our forefathers worshiped God on this mountain, but others say that we must worship in the temple."

12. Jesus said to her, "Truly I tell you, the day is coming when neither on this mountain nor in the temple will you worship the Father.

13. "But the day is coming and is now here when the true worshipers of God will worship the Father in spirit and in truth, for these are the only worshipers God desires.

14. "God is spirit, and those who worship God must do so in spirit and in truth."

15. Then the woman said to Him, "I know that Messiah is coming (he who is called Christ); when he comes, he will show us all things."

16. Jesus said to her, "I am that one who speaks to you."

17. Now, His disciples came back from town, and they were amazed that He was speaking with a woman, yet no one said, "What do You want with her," or "Why were You speaking with her."

18. So, the woman left her water jug and rushed into the town and said to the men, "Come, see a man who told me all the things I have ever done; could this be the Christ?"

19. Therefore, they came out of the town and were coming to Him.

20. Meanwhile, the disciples were saying to Him, "Teacher, You must eat," but He said to them, "I have food to eat that you do not know about."

21. So the disciples asked of one another, "Did anyone bring Him food to eat?"

22. Jesus said to them, "My food is to do the will of Him who sent Me and to accomplish His work.

23. "Do you not say there is yet a season and then we will start the harvest? Behold, I tell you, look at the fields as they are right now. They are ripe for the harvest.

24. "Already the one who reaps is gathering his wages and gathering fruit for life eternal, so that he who reaps and he who sows may rejoice together. For in this case it is true that one sows and another reaps.

25. "I sent you to reap what you have not labored for. Others have labored and you have entered into their labor."

26. From the town, many of the people believed because of the testimony of the woman who said, "He told me all the things I have ever done."

27. So when they came to Jesus, they asked Him to stay with them, and He stayed there two more days, and many more believed His word.

28. And then when the Word came upon them, they said to the woman, "It is not for what you said that we believe, for we have heard His words for ourselves and know that this One is indeed the savior of the world."

CHAPTER 11

1. Then Jesus and His disciples crossed a large lake in a boat, and when they arrived at the other side of the lake, a large crowd began to gather, so Jesus stayed by the lakeshore.

2. At that time, one of the religious leaders came to Him, and upon seeing Him, fell before Him at His feet and implored Him saying, "My little daughter, my only child, is at the point of death; please come and lay Your hands on her, and she will get well and live."

3. So Jesus went off with him, and a large crowd followed Jesus and pressed in on Him.

4. In that crowd, there was a woman who had an issue of bleeding for twelve years, and suffered much at the hands of physicians, and spent all she had and was not helped at all, but was made even worse.

5. After hearing about Jesus, she came up behind Him in the crowd and touched His clothes, for she said to herself, "If I just touch even His clothes, I will get well."

6. Immediately, the flow of her blood dried up, and she felt in her body that she was healed of her disease.

7. But Jesus perceived that the power within Him had gone forth from Him, so He turned around in the crowed and asked, "Who touched My clothes?" But all the people denied it.

8. And His disciples said to Him, "You see the crowd all around You and yet You ask, 'Who touched My clothes?'"

9. Still Jesus looked for the one who had touched Him.

10. And the woman was in fear and was trembling, for she was aware of what had happened to her. So, she fell at Jesus' feet and told Him the whole truth.

11. And He said to her, "Daughter, your faith has made you well; go in peace and be healed of your disease."

12. While He was speaking to her, they came out of the house of the religious leader and said, "Your daughter has died; why trouble the Teacher any longer?"

13. But Jesus overheard what was being said to the religious leader and said to him, "No longer be afraid; just believe."

14. And as He approached the house, Jesus allowed only the religious leader, his wife, Peter, James, and John (the brother of James) to go with Him to see the young girl.

15. And many came out of the house weeping and wailing for the loss of the girl, but Jesus said to them, "Why all the commotion? The girl is not dead, she is only sleeping."

16. At that they began to laugh at Him, but He put them all out of the house and took along the child's father and mother, and His companions, and they entered the room where the girl was.

17. Taking the girl's hand, He said to her, "Get up."

18. And immediately the spirit returned to the girl, who was twelve years old, and she got up and began to walk about, and all in the room were astounded at the miracle.

19. But Jesus gave them strict orders that no one should know about this. Then He told them to give her food to eat.

20. Thereafter, Jesus was going through the land with His disciples teaching in the temples and proclaiming the Gospel of the kingdom of God. He healed every kind of disease and sickness among the people, and the news about Him spread rapidly, and large crowds began to follow Him everywhere.

21. In one town, a military officer came to Jesus imploring Him saying, "My servant is lying paralyzed at home and is tormented and afraid of his condition."

22. Jesus said to him, "I will come and heal him."

23. But the officer said, "Lord, I am not worthy for You to enter my home, but if You just say the word, my servant will be healed. Because, I too am a man under authority, and I have soldiers under me. If I say to one, 'Do this,' or 'Do that.' I know that it will be done."

24. When Jesus heard this, He marveled at the officer's faith and said, "Truly, I have not encountered such faith in all this land.

25. "I tell you that many will come to Me from the East and West and recline with Me at My Father's table while many for whom the kingdom was created will be cast into the outer darkness where there is nothing but weeping and gnashing of teeth."

26. So, Jesus said to the officer, "Go, and it shall be done for you as you have believed." And the officer's servant was healed at that moment.

CHAPTER 12

1. After these things, there was a feast for the people, and Jesus went up to Jerusalem.

2. Now, in Jerusalem, there is a bathing pool by the sheep gate, which is called Bethesda pool, and it has five porches beside it.

3. Upon these laid a multitude of those who were sick, blind, lame, and withered; and they waited there for a stirring of the waters for it was said that an angel of the Lord went down at a certain season into the pool and stirred up the water.

4. Whoever was first to step in after the stirring of the water was made well from whatever disease afflicted them.

5. There was a man there who had been ill for thirty-eight years, and when Jesus saw him there, and knew that he had already been a long time in that condition, He said to him, "Do you want to be healed."

6. But the sick man answered Him, "Sir, I have no one to put me in the pool when the water stirs, so while I am trying to get in, another person gets in before me."

7. So, Jesus said to him, "Get up. Pick up your mat and walk."

8. Immediately, the man became well, picked up his mat and began to walk. Now that day was the sabbath when none were allowed to work.

9. So the religious leaders were saying to the man, "It is the sabbath, and you are not permitted to carry your mat."

10. But he said to them, "He who made me well was the one who told me to pick up my mat and walk."

11. Then they asked him, "Who told you to do this?"

12. But the man who had been healed did not know who it was that healed him, for Jesus had slipped away into the crowd.

13. Afterward, Jesus found him in the temple and said to him, "Behold, you have become well; stop sinning so that nothing worse happens to you."

14. The man went away and told the religious leaders that it was Jesus who had healed him.

15. So the religious leaders persecuted Jesus for doing these things on the sabbath, but He answered them, "My Father is working even now, and I, Myself, am working."

16. Because of this, the religious leaders and those who follow them were seeking to kill Jesus. He was breaking the sabbath, but worse to them, He was calling God His father and therefore making Himself equal to God.

17. But Jesus answered them saying, "Truly, I tell you, the Son can do nothing of Himself unless He sees the Father doing it. For whatever the Father does, the Son does in the same manner.

18. "For the Father loves the Son and shows Him all things that He Himself is doing. And the Father will show Him greater works than these, so that you will marvel.

19. "For just as the Father raises the dead and gives them life, so to the Son gives life to whomever He wishes.

20. "The Father judges no one, but has given all judgment to the Son, so that all will honor the Son, even as they honor the Father who sent Him.

21. "Truly I tell you, anyone who hears My word, and believes in Him who sent Me, has eternal life and does not come into judgment, but rather has passed out of death into life.

22. "Truly I tell you, an hour is coming, and has now come, when the dead will hear the voice of the Son of God and those who hear that voice will live.

23. "For just as the Father has life in Himself, even so He gave to the Son to have life within Himself, and He gave Him authority to execute judgment.

24. "But do not marvel at this; for a time is coming when all who are in the tombs will hear His voice and will come out—those who did good works to a resurrection of life, but those whose works were evil to a resurrection of judgment.

25. "I can do nothing on My own initiative; As I hear, I judge; and My judgment is just, because I do not seek My own will, but rather the will of Him who sent Me.

26. "You went to the wilderness and inquired of John the Baptist. He was the lamp that was burning, and you were willing to rejoice in his light for a time, but he has testified to the truth about Me.

27. "And there is another who testifies of Me, and I know that the testimony which He gives about Me is true. For the testimony which I receive is not from man, but I say these things so that you may be saved.

28. "For this testimony is greater than that of John the Baptist's. It is the works the Father has given Me to accomplish—the very works that I do testify about Me, and that is that the Father has indeed sent Me.

29. "And though the Father sending Me testifies about Me, you neither hear His voice, nor have you ever seen His form, for you do not have His word abiding in you. And you do not have His word abiding in you, because you do not believe in Him who He sent.

30. "So, you search the scriptures thinking that in them you will gain eternal life; and yet it is these which testify about Me. How sad it is then that you are unwilling to come to Me and live.

31. "Yet My glory is not given to Me from mankind. For people do not have the love of God within them.

32. "I come in My Father's name and you do not receive Me, but if another comes in their own name— that person you will receive.

33. "How can you believe, when you accept glory from one another and never seek the glory that is from the one and only God?

34. "But do not think that I will accuse you before the Father; the one who accuses you is the very scriptures you revere and set your hope upon. For if you believed those scriptures, you would believe in Me—because they are about Me.

35. "But if you do not believe in the words you claim are true, how will you believe My words?"

CHAPTER 13

1. Then one day by the sea, He began to teach and such a large crowd formed to listen that He got into a boat and pushed off from the shore and taught them as they waited by the sea on the land.

2. And He taught them many things in parables, and this He said to them in His teaching:

3. "The sower went out to sow, and as he did, some seeds fell beside the road and the birds came and ate them up.

4. "Other seed fell on rocky ground where it had little soil, and immediately it sprang up, because it had no depth of soil beneath it. And when the sun had risen, it scorched the plant; and because it had no root it withered away.

5. "Other seeds fell among the thorns, and the thorns came up and choked them, and they yielded no crop at all.

6. "Other seeds fell into good soil, and they grew strong and increased their yield, some thirty, some sixty, and some a hundredfold.

7. "To those who have ears to hear, let them hear."

8. As soon as He was alone some of His disciples began asking Him about the parable. And Mary (of Magdalene) asked the Lord, "Are You addressing this parable to only us, or to all people?"

9. And He said to them, "To you it has been granted to know the mysteries of the kingdom of God, but to them it has not been granted, and those who are outside hear everything in parables, so that while seeing with their eyes, they see nothing, and while hearing with their ears, they understand nothing.

10. "For the heart of these people have become dull, otherwise they would turn and I would heal them."

11. And He said to them, "Do you not understand this parable? If you do not understand this parable, how will you ever understand any other?

12. "Nevertheless, blessed are your eyes because they see; and your ears because they can hear. For truly I tell you that many prophets and righteous men desired to see what you see and did not. They desired to hear what you can hear and never heard it."

13. Then Jesus explained, "The sower sows the word of God.

14. "When the word falls on those beside the road, they hear the word, but do not understand it. Therefore, Satan comes at once and steals it away so they will not believe and be saved.

15. "When the word falls on those in the rocky places, they immediately receive it with joy, but they have no root in themselves, and as soon as persecution arises because of the word, or temptations come, they immediately fall away.

16. "Others are those who are among the thorns when the word comes to them, but the worries of the world, the deceitfulness of riches, the pleasures of this life, and the desire for other things choke the word, and it brings forth no fruit to maturity.

17. "But the ones who are the good soil where the word is sown, hear it and accept it in an honest and good heart and bear fruit with it, some thirty, some sixty, and some even a hundred fold."

18. Then Jesus taught them in the following manner: "Do not lie, and do not do what you hate, for all things are disclosed before heaven.

19. "For a lamp is not brought to be put under a basket, but rather to be set on a table, and nothing is hidden that is not intended to be revealed; There is nothing secret that will not come to light. If anyone has ears to hear, let them hear this.

20. "And take care how you listen. By your standard of measure, it will be measured out to you, and more will be given to you as well, because to whomever has more will be given, but to him who has not, even what he has will be taken away."

21. And then He said to them, "How shall we picture the kingdom of God? What parable will describe it?

22. "It's like a man who casts seed upon the soil and goes to bed, and when he awakes in the day, the seed sprouts and grows—how it does so is a mystery to him.

23. "The soil produces the crop all by itself; first the blade, then the head, then the whole grain in the head, and when the crop is ready, the man immediately gathers it to himself, for the harvest has come.

24. "The kingdom is like a mustard seed which when sown upon the soil is the smallest of seeds, but it grows to become the largest of all the plants in the garden, and its branches grow large enough for the birds of the air to nest within its shade."

25. With such parables, Jesus spoke his words to the people, as much as they were able to hear it. And He did not speak to the masses without a parable, but would always, in private, explain the meaning to His disciples.

26. For as He said, "I disclose my mysteries only to those who are worthy." And with His mouth, He uttered things hidden since the foundation of the world.

27. And He spoke to the people in another parable saying, "The kingdom of heaven is like a man who sowed good seed in his field.

28. "But while his workers were sleeping, his enemy came and sowed tares among the wheat and went away.

29. "When the wheat sprang up and bore grain, the tares sprang up as well.

30. "The workers came to the landowner and said, 'Sir, did you not sow good seed in your field? How is it that tares have grown in as well?'

31. "And he said to them, 'An enemy has done this.'

32. "The workers asked, 'Shall we dig up the tares?' But he said to them, 'No, for you will injure the wheat as well. Allow both to grow together until harvest time.

33. And in the time of harvest, the tares will be conspicuous, and I will order that first the tares be gathered up in bundles and burned, but the wheat to be gathered up and put into my barn.'"

34. Then Jesus left and went into the house, and His disciples came to Him and asked Him to explain the parable of the tares.

35. And He said to them, "The one who sows the good seed is the Son of Man, and the field is the world; and as for the good seed, these are the children of the kingdom; the tares are the children of the evil one, and the enemy who sowed the tares is Satan. The harvest is the end of the age, and the reapers are angels.

36. "So, just as the tares are gathered up and burned, so shall it be for the sons of Satan at the end of the age.

37. "The Son of Man will send out His angels to gather out all stumbling blocks and those who do lawlessness and will throw them into the fire, and in that place will be great weeping and gnashing of teeth.

38. "And then the righteous will shine in the kingdom of their Father. Let the one who has ears hear this word."

CHAPTER 14

1. At another time, Jesus and His disciples were walking through the wheat fields on the sabbath and His disciples became hungry and began to pick the heads of grain and rubbed them in their hands and ate the grain.

2. But when the religious leaders saw this, they complained to Jesus saying, "Look at how Your disciples sin by doing what is unlawful to do on the sabbath."

3. So, He said to them, "How can it be that My disciples sin by working on the sabbath, and yet you make your entire living by working on the holy day? But these sins you speak of come from your traditions.

4. "And now I tell you that something greater than tradition has arrived.

5. "But if you ever knew God or the one whom He sent, then you would know that He requires compassion and not sacrifice. If you knew this, then you would not condemn the innocent. For the sabbath was made for man, not man for the sabbath.

6. "And now the Son of Man is Lord, even of the sabbath."

7. Departing from there, He went into the Church, and a man was there whose hand was withered, and they questioned Jesus so they might entrap Him saying, "Is it lawful then to heal on the sabbath?" For the practice of healing was not permitted on that day.

8. And He said to them, "Who among you if they have a sheep and it falls into a ditch on the sabbath would not work to free it and bring it up? Is a man not as valuable as a sheep?

9. "So then, is it lawful to do good on the sabbath—to save a life or destroy it?" But they all remained silent.

10. Then He said to the man, "Get up and come forward." And he got up and came to Jesus.

11. Then Jesus looked with anger at all the people who were judging Him, and He grieved at the hardness of their hearts.

12. Then He said to the man, "Stretch out your hand."

13. The man stretched out his hand and immediately it was cured and made whole like his other hand.

14. But the religious people and their leaders were enraged, and the leaders went out and conspired against Him, scheming at the highest levels as to how they might destroy Him.

15. Jesus, aware of their motives, withdrew and many followed Him and He healed them all on that Sabbath.

16. And whenever the unclean spirits saw Him, they would fall down before Him and shout, "You are the Son of God!" but He warned them all to tell no one who He was.

17. Later, a demon-possessed man who was blind and mute was brought to Jesus and He healed him, so that the mute spoke and saw.

18. All the people were amazed and were asking, "Could this man be the Son of God?"

19. But when the religious leaders heard this, they said among themselves, "This man casts out demons by the power of Satan, the father of demons."

20. And Jesus, who knew their thoughts, said to them, "Any kingdom divided against itself is destroyed by itself, and any city or any house divided against itself will fall.

21. "Or how can anyone enter the strong man's house and carry off his property, unless he first binds the strong man? And then he will plunder his house.

22. "When a strong man guards his own house, his possessions are safe.

23. "But when someone stronger than he attacks and overpowers him, then he strips him of all his armor and steals all his possessions.

24. "If Satan casts out Satan, he is divided against himself; how then can his kingdom stand? And if it is by Satan that I cast out demons, how is it that you religious leaders cast them out? Indeed, for this reason, they will be your judges.

25. "But if I cast out demons by the Spirit of God, then the kingdom of God has come upon you.

26. "Know this: The one who is not with Me is against Me; and the one who does not gather with Me, scatters.

27. "For this reason, I say to you that all sin and blasphemy a person does will be forgiven of that person, but blasphemy against the Spirit will not be forgiven. That person is guilty of an eternal sin.

28. "Whoever speaks against the Son of Man shall be forgiven, but whoever speaks against the Holy Spirit—the Spirit of Truth—will never be forgiven, not now and not in the future."

29. As Jesus set out to leave that area, a rich young ruler of the people ran up to Him and kneeled before Him, and asked, "Good Teacher, what can I do to inherit eternal life?"

30. And Jesus said to him, "Why do you call me good? No one is good except for God alone.

31. "But you know the commandments: Do not murder; do not commit adultery; do not steal; do not bear false witness; do not defraud others; honor your father and mother."

32. And the man said to Him, "I have kept all of these commandments since I was a child."

33. And Jesus, looking at him, felt compassion for him and said, "There is one thing you lack that keeps you incomplete: Go and sell all you have and give it all away, and you will have treasure in heaven. Then come and follow Me."

34. At this, the young ruler felt sad and grieved as he left, for he was very wealthy.

35. And Jesus, looking around, said to His followers, "How hard it will be for those who are wealthy to enter the kingdom of heaven.

36. "I tell you, it is easier for a camel to go through the eye of a needle than for a rich person to enter the kingdom of God."

37. His disciples were astonished and said to Him, "Then who can ever be saved?"

38. Jesus replied, "With mankind this is impossible, but with God, all things are possible."

39. Then Peter said to Him, "We have left everything and followed You; what will there be for us?"

40. Jesus said, "Truly I tell you, no one who has left their home, or brothers and sisters, or mother, or children for My sake and the sake of the Gospel will fail to receive a hundred times as much in this present age.

41. "They will gain houses, brothers, sisters, mothers, children and also persecutions; and in the age to come—eternal life.

42. "Surely, you will sit on thrones beside Me and judge the entire world. And if you hear My words and do them, the very stones of the earth will serve you.

43. "But many who are first will be last, and the last, first."

CHAPTER 15

1. Jesus asked His disciples, "Who do the people say the Son of Man is?"

2. And they said, "Some say You are John the Baptist. Others say You are a prophet. Still others say You are the return of Elijah or Jeremiah."

3. "But who do you say that I am?"

4. Peter answered saying, "You are the Christ, the Son of the Living God."

5. And Jesus said to him, "Blessed are you, Peter. For flesh and blood has not revealed this to you, but My Father in heaven has done so. And I say to you that upon that rock I will build My church—and the gates of hell will not prevail against it.

6. "To you, I will give the keys to the kingdom of heaven, and whatever you bind on earth will be bound in heaven, and whatever you let loose on earth will be let loose in heaven."

7. Then He warned them all to tell no one that He was the Christ.

8. He asked them again, "Compare me to something and tell me what I am like."

9. And Peter said, "You are like a messenger."

10. Matthew said, "You are like a wise philosopher."

11. But Thomas said to Him, "Teacher, my mouth is utterly unable to say what you are like."

12. Jesus said, "Then I am not your teacher. Rather, you have drunk from and become intoxicated by the bubbling spring that I have tended."

13. Then Jesus took Thomas aside and spoke three things to him, and when they returned, the others asked Thomas what Jesus had said.

14. But he said to them, "If I tell you even one of the sayings He spoke to me, you will pick up rocks to stone me, and fire will come from those rocks and consume you."

15. From that time, Jesus began to show His followers that He must go to the Jerusalem and suffer many things from the elders and chief priests, and then He must be killed, but after three days, He was to rise again.

16. He was stating the matter plainly, but Peter took Him aside and began to chastise Him, saying, "This will never happen to You. You must not let it happen."

17. But He said to Peter, "Get behind me, Satan! You are a stumbling block to Me; you are not setting your mind on God's will but on human desire."

18. Then Jesus turned to His disciples and said, "If anyone wishes to come after me, they must deny themselves and take up their cross and follow Me daily.

19. "For anyone who wishes to save their life will lose it; but whoever loses their life for My sake and that of the Gospel will find it.

20. "What does it profit a person to gain the entire world and forfeit their very soul, or what can a person give in exchange for their soul?

21. "For the Son of Man is going to come in God's glory with the angels and will repay everyone according to their deeds. And whoever is ashamed of Me and My word in this adulterous and sinful generation, the Son of Man will be ashamed of that person before the Father.

22. "Truly I tell you, there are some of those who are standing here right now who will not taste death until they see the Son of Man coming in His kingdom."

CHAPTER 16

1. Later, they came across a man born blind from birth, and His disciples asked Him, "Teacher, who sinned? Was it this man or was it his parent's sin that caused him to be born blind?"

2. Jesus answered, "It was not for this man's sin nor the sins of his parent's that he was born blind, but rather so the works of God might be made manifest in him."

3. "We must work the works of Him who sent Me as long as there is daylight. For the night is approaching when no one can work.

4. "While I am in the world, I am the Light of the world."

5. When He had said this, He knelt down and spit in the dirt to make a mudpack, and He placed the mud on the blind man's eyelids and said to him, "Go wash in the fountain."

6. So he went away and washed in the public fountain and came back seeing.

7. Therefore, the man's neighbors and those who had witnessed him begging in the streets were saying, "Is not this the man who used to sit and beg?"

8. Others were saying, "Surely, this is he." But others were saying, "No, it is only someone who looks like him." But the man who was originally born blind continued to say, "I am the one."

9. So, they said to him, "How then were your eyes opened?"

10. And he said to them, "Jesus made a mudpack and anointed my eyes, and said to me, 'Go to the public fountain and wash.'; so I went away and washed, and I gained my sight."

11. Then they said to him, "Where is this Jesus?" But he answered them, "I do not know."

12. So, they brought the man who was formerly blind to the Pharisees, and again it was the sabbath when Jesus had made the mudpack and opened his eyes.

13. The religious leaders began to question the man and asked, "How did you receive your sight?" And he said to them, "He applied a mudpack to my eyes; then I washed, and now I see."

14. Some of the religious leaders said, "This Jesus is not from God, because He does not obey the rules of the sabbath." But others said, "How can a sinner perform such signs and wonders."

15. And they asked the former blind man, "What do you say about Him, since He opened your eyes?"

16. And the man said, "Surely, He is a prophet."

17. The religious leaders stopped believing that the man had even been born blind to begin with, until they called the parents of this very one who had received his sight.

18. And they questioned them saying, "Is this your son, who you say was born blind? If so, then how does he now see?"

19. His parents answered the leaders and said, "We know that this is our son, and that he was born blind, but we do not know how he can now see. But why do you not ask him? He is of age."

20. His parents said, "He is of age; ask him," because they knew that the religious leaders had agreed that whoever said Jesus was the Christ, would be thrown out of the Church.

21. So, a second time, they called the man who had been born blind and said to him, "Praise God, and then admit that this Jesus is a sinner."

22. He answered them and said, "Whether or not He is a sinner, I do not know, but I do know that where once I was blind, now I can see."

23. So they asked, "What did He do? How did He open your eyes?"

24. The man said to them, "I already told you once, and you did not listen; why do you want to hear the same story again? Do you want to become His disciples, as well?"

25. Then they reviled him and said, "You are His disciple, but we are disciples of Moses. We know that God spoke to the Moses, but we do not even know where this Jesus is from."

26. The man responded by saying, "This is an amazing thing. You are the priests, yet you do not know where Jesus is from, and yet He opened my eyes. We know that God does not hear from sinners; but if anyone is God-fearing and does His will, He hears them.

27. "Since the beginning of time it has never been heard of that anyone restored the sight of a person born blind. If Jesus were not from God, He could do nothing."

28. But the religious leaders replied, "You were born in sin and are steeped in it, and yet you are teaching us?"

29. Then, from the temple, they cast out the man who could now see.

30. When Jesus heard that they had cast him out, and when He found him, He asked, "Do you believe in the Son of Man?"

31. He answered, "Who is He Lord—that I might believe in Him?"

32. Jesus said, "You have seen Him, and He is the one who is talking with you now."

33. And the man who now saw everything clearly replied, "Yes, Lord, I do believe."

34. Then Jesus said, "For judgment I came into the word, so those who do not see may see, and those who see become blind."

35. Some of the religious leaders heard Him say this and said to Him, "Surely, we are not blind."

36. But Jesus replied, "If you were blind, you'd be free from sin, but since you claim to see, your sin remains."

CHAPTER 17

1. Then Jesus spoke this parable to the religious leaders, "A man who enters the barn in any way other than the door is a thief and has come to steal the sheep.

2. "The shepherd of the sheep enters through the door. The doorkeeper opens the door and lets the shepherd in, and the sheep hear the shepherd's voice, and he leads them out.

3. "Then when he has led them out, he walks in front of them and leads them to pasture, and they follow him, because they recognize his voice.

4. "The sheep will not follow a stranger, because they do not recognize his voice; instead, they will run away."

5. This parable Jesus spoke to them, but they did not understand what He was telling them, so He spoke more plainly.

6. "I am the door for the sheep. All who came before Me are thieves and robbers, but the sheep did not hear them.

7. "I am the door; if anyone enters through Me, that person will be saved, and they will go in and out and find pasture.

8. "The thief comes to kill, steal, and destroy, but I have come that they may have life and have that life more abundantly.

9. "I am the good shepherd, and the shepherd lays down His life for the sheep.

10. "The hired hand, who is not the owner, sees the wolf coming for the sheep and runs away; then the wolf snatches the sheep and the flock is scattered. He flees, because he is the hired hand and has no real concern for the sheep.

11. "I am the good shepherd, and I know My own, and My own know Me, even as the Father knows Me and I know the Father, and I lay My life down for the sheep.

12. "I have other sheep, which are not of this fold. And I must gather them also, and they will hear My voice and will become one with the flock and have one shepherd.

13. "For this reason the Father loves Me, because I lay down My life so that I may take it up again.

14. "No one has taken it from Me, but I lay it down by My own will. I have authority to lay it down, and I have authority to take it up again. This is the commandment I received from My Father."

15. So a division occurred among the religious leaders because of these words Jesus spoke. Many were saying, "He has a demon and is insane. Why do you listen to Him?"

16. Others were saying, "These sayings are not the sayings of a demon-possessed person."

17. Some time later, in the winter, during the religious feast being hosted in Jerusalem, Jesus was walking among the grounds of the temple and the council of the elders of the people, both the chief priests and scribes encircled Him and were saying to Him, "How long will You keep us in suspense? If You are the Christ, tell us plainly."

18. Jesus answered them, "I told you, and yet you do not believe. The works that I do in My Father's name testify about Me.

19. "But you do not believe in Me, because you are not My sheep. My sheep hear My voice and they know Me, and they follow Me, and to them I give eternal life so they will never perish, and no one can snatch them from My hand.

20. "My Father who has given them to Me is greater than all; and no one is able to snatch them from the Father's hand.

21. "I and the Father are one."

22. At that, the religious leaders became enraged and picked up stones to kill Him, but Jesus said to them, "I showed you many good works from the Father, for which one are you stoning Me?"

23. The religious leaders said, "We are not going to stone You for any good works but rather because You being a man make Yourself out to be God."

24. Jesus answered them, "From your own scriptures, you say 'you are gods,' how can you stone the one whom the Father

has sanctified and sent into the world because I say I and the Father are one and that I am the Son of God?

25. "If I do not do the works of the Father, do not believe Me; but if I do them, even though you may not believe Me, believe in the works so that you may come to know and understand that the Father is in Me, and I am in the Father."

26. But they went to seize Jesus anyway, yet He eluded their grasp.

27. And Jesus went far away then to the place where John the Baptist was first baptizing people before his arrest, and He remained there for some time.

28. Many came to Him in that place and realized that what John the Baptist had said about Him was true. And many believed in Christ in that place.

CHAPTER 18

1. The disciples of John the Baptist reported to John all these things, and summoning two of his disciples, John sent them to the Lord saying, "Are You the one we were waiting for, or should we look further?"

2. When they came to Jesus they asked him John's question, and He answered them saying, "Go report to John what you have seen and heard: the blind receive sight; the lame walk; lepers are cleansed; the deaf hear; the dead are raised to life, and the poor have the Gospel preached to them."

3. When the messengers of John the Baptist had left, Jesus began to speak to the crowds about John.

4. "What did you go out into the wilderness to find, a reed shaken by the wind? Or what did you go out to see, a man dressed in soft clothing? Those who wear fine clothes live in palaces.

5. "But what did you go out to see? A prophet? Yes, a prophet, and even more than a prophet. For this is the one who foretold you about Me. He is the messenger who prepared the way for Me.

6. "In truth, there has been none greater born among women than John. And yet, I say to you, those who are least in the kingdom of God are greater than John the Baptist.

7. "From the days of John the Baptist until now, the kingdom of heaven has suffered violence and violent people take it by force. For all the prophets and the law prophesied about me until John, and if you are willing to accept it, he is the Elijah who was to come. Whoever has ears, let them hear.

8. "But what good were the prophets? And to what shall I compare this generation of humankind who benefited from them? They are like children who sit in the market place calling out to one another saying, 'We played a flute for you and you did not dance; we sang a dirge and you did not weep.'

9. "For John came drinking no wine and fasting much and they said, 'He has a demon!' The Son of Man has come eating and drinking and they say, 'Behold, a glutton and a drunkard—a friend to the sinners!'

10. "Yet wisdom is proved in the deeds that people do."

11. And King Herod heard of all this, for Jesus and what He preached had become very well known, and the people were saying, "John the Baptist has risen from the dead, and that is why these miraculous powers are at work in Him."

12. Still others were saying he was an old prophet risen again, but when Herod heard all this, he kept saying "John, whom I beheaded, is risen!"

13. For Herod himself had sent and had John arrested and bound in prison on account of Herodias, the wife of his brother whom Herod had taken and married.

14. John had been saying publicly, "It is not lawful for you to take your brother's wife!"

15. And for that reason, Herodias had a grudge against John and wanted him put to death, and yet she could not convince Herod to do so.

16. Herod was afraid of John, knowing that he was a righteous and holy man, and he kept him safe, even while he was in prison. And when he heard John calling out and preaching from his cell, he was perplexed, but he enjoyed listening to him all the same.

17. Then came Herod's birthday and he threw a large banquet for all his lords and military commanders, and all the leading men in the land.

18. And when the daughter of Herodias came and danced for Herod, by his request, she pleased him so much that he said to the girl, "Ask whatever you will as payment and you shall have it—even if it is half of my kingdom."

19. So, the girl went out and asked her mother what to ask for, and Herodias told her to ask for the head of John the Baptist.

20. Immediately she came in to the king and said, "I want you to give me at once the head of John the Baptist on a platter."

21. And though it greatly grieved the king, he was unwilling to lose honor among his dinner guests and friends, and so he had the executioner take John and behead him.

22. The head was brought on a platter to the girl, and she took it and gave it to her mother.

23. When the disciples heard about this, they came and took away John's body and laid it in a tomb.

24. Jesus' disciples then went and told Jesus all that had occurred and He said to them, "Come away by yourselves to a secluded place and rest a while" (For the crowds were constantly coming to Jesus and His followers.). So they went away in a boat to a secluded place by themselves.

CHAPTER 19

1. After these things, Jesus went away to the other side of the sea. A large crowd followed Him, because they saw the signs that He was performing on those who were sick.

2. For this reason, Jesus went up on a mountain, and there He sat down with His disciples. And seeing another large crowd gathering, He felt compassion for them, for they were like sheep without a shepherd.

3. So He healed the sick among them, and then said to Philip as the evening was approaching, "Where are we to buy food to feed all these people?"

4. He said this to test Philip, because He already knew what He was going to do.

5. Philip answered and said, "This is a desolate place. We should send them away into the towns and villages so they can find food to eat. Even two hundred gold coins are not

enough to buy food for all these people—even if all had only a little to eat."

6. "Philip," Jesus said, "They, do not need to go away; you give them something to eat."

7. Then Andrew said to Jesus, "There is a boy here who has five loaves of bread and two fish, but what are these for so many people?"

8. Jesus said, "Have the people sit down." There was much grass in the area, and the people sat in groups of fifty and one hundred and they numbered about five thousand, not including all the children who were with them.

9. Jesus then took the loaves, and after looking to heaven and blessing the food, He distributed the food to His disciples who then distributed it to those who were seated.

10. He distributed the fish as well in the same manner, and all who were there ate as much as they wanted.

11. And when they were filled, He said to His disciples, "Gather up the leftovers, so that nothing is wasted."

12. So they gathered them up and filled twelve baskets full from the original five loaves and two fish.

13. And when the people saw this sign that He had done, they said, "Surely this is a prophet of God who has come into the world."

14. After this, He made His disciples get into a boat and go ahead of Him to the other side of the sea. Then He sent the crowd on their way.

15. And after He sent the crowds away, He went up on a mountain by Himself to pray in the evening.

16. The disciples in the boat began to encounter a storm, and the wind tossed the sea about, and they began to fear for their lives.

17. Then, late in the night during the storm, the disciples saw Jesus coming to them, walking over the waves on the surface of the water, and He intended to pass by them.

18. But they were terrified for they were certain they were seeing a ghost.

19. And they cried out in terror, but Jesus spoke to them saying, "Have courage; it is I."

20. So, Peter said to Him, "Lord, if it is really You, command me to come to You on the water."

21. Jesus said to him, "Come unto Me."

22. At that, Peter got out of the boat and walked on the surface of the water and came toward Jesus. But seeing the storm and the waves, he became frightened, and then he began to sink.

23. Peter cried out, "Lord, save me!"

24. And immediately, Jesus stretched out His hand and took hold of him and said, "You of little faith; why did you doubt?"

25. When they got into the boat, the other disciples cried out "Teacher, do You not care that we are about to die!"

26. So, He stood in the bow of the boat and rebuked the wind and the sea saying, "Hush; be still," and suddenly the wind stopped and the waves became still.

27. And Jesus said to them all, "Why are you so afraid? Even after the loaves and fishes, do you still have no faith?"

28. And then the boat was instantly on the other side of the sea sitting on the shore. And those who were in the boat worshiped Jesus saying, "You must be the Son of God."

29. When the people of that place recognized Him, they sent word into all the surrounding areas, and all who were sick were brought to Him.

30. And they begged Him that they may just touch the fringe of His garments; and as many as touched it were cured.

CHAPTER 20

1. Sometime later, Jesus called His disciples together and gave them power and authority over all the demons and to heal all diseases.

2. And these were His twelve disciples: Peter, Andrew, James, Mary, and John; Philip, Bartholomew, Thomas, Matthew, Thaddeus, Simon and Judas.

3. And also there were other women following who had been cured of evil spirits, Joanna and Susanna, and many others who were contributing to the support of the group from their private means.

4. So He sent them out in pairs to proclaim the kingdom of God and to perform healings.

5. He said to them, "Freely you have received; now freely give.

6. "For the harvest is plentiful, but the laborers are few. Therefore beseech the lord of the harvest to send out the laborers into his fields.

7. "Take nothing for your journey. Do not take a staff or bag, or food or money, and do not even have a change of clothes. For the worker is worthy of support.

8. "Whatever house you enter, determine first that it is worthy, and then stay there until you leave that city.

9. "If the house is worthy, give it your blessing of peace, but if it is not, take away your blessing of peace.

10. "And as for those who do not receive you, as you go from that town, shake the dust off your feet as a testimony against them.

11. "Know that the one who listens to you, listens to Me, and the one who rejects you, rejects Me; and those who reject Me reject the Father who sent Me.

12. "Behold, I send you out as sheep among wolves; therefore be wise as serpents and innocent as doves, and proclaim that the kingdom of God has come to them.

13. "And know that those who do not receive your testimony will receive the judgment of the damned.

14. "As you go, beware; for they will hand you over to be tried and persecuted. And they will condemn you in their synagogues on account of Me.

15. "You will even be brought before kings and governors for My sake, as a testimony to them.

16. "But when they hand you over, do not worry what you will say or how you will say it. For it will be given to you in that hour what you are to say.

17. "For it is not you who speaks, but it is the Father who speaks through you."

18. And as the disciples left, they began going through the villages preaching the Gospel and healing the afflicted.

19. When the apostles returned, they gave an account to Him of all they had done. And they reported with joy, "Lord, even the demons are subject to Your name."

20. And Jesus said, "I was watching Satan fall from heaven like lightning. For behold, I have given you authority to tread on serpents and scorpions and over all the power of the enemy, and nothing will injure you.

21. "Nevertheless, do not rejoice that the spirits are subject to you, rather rejoice that your names are written in heaven."

22. At that time, Jesus rejoiced in the Holy Spirit and said, "I praise You, O Father, Lord of heaven and earth, that You have hidden these things from the learned and have revealed them to the infants. Yes, Father, for this way was well pleasing in Your sight.

23. Then He said to the twelve, "All things have been handed over to Me by My Father, and no one knows who the Son is except the Father, and who the Father is except for the Son—and anyone to whom the Son reveals Him."

24. Then they came to the other side of the sea to the countryside.

25. When Jesus got out of the boat, a man with an unclean spirit who lived among the tombs came to Him.

26. The man had often been bound with shackles and chains, but he broke them all, and no one was able to bind him any longer, because they were not strong enough.

27. Constantly, night and day, he screamed among the tombs and cut himself with stones and other sharp objects. And no one could pass by that way on account of him.

28. But seeing Jesus from a distance, he ran up and bowed before Him, and shouting with a loud voice he said, "What business do we have with each other, Jesus, Son of the Most High God? I beg You, in the name of God, do not torment me!"

29. But Jesus said to the demon within the man, "Come out of him!" and then asked it, "What is your name?"

30. And the demon said, "My name is Legion, for we are many." And the demon begged Jesus not to send them out of the country and into the abyss.

31. Now there was a large herd of swine feeding nearby on the mountain, and the demon implored Jesus saying, "Send us into the swine so that we may enter them."

32. Jesus gave permission, and coming out, the unclean spirits entered the swine, but the herd rushed down the steep bank into the sea, about two thousand in all, and they all drowned themselves in the sea.

33. The herdsman of the swine ran away and reported it in the village, and the people came to see what it was that had happened.

34. They came to Jesus and observed the man who had been possessed. The man was sitting down, clothed and in his right mind—the very man who had the legion of demons—and they all became frightened.

35. Those who had witnessed the sign Jesus performed told all about the demon-possessed man and the swine. So the people of the area began to implore Jesus to leave the area.

36. So, as He was getting back into the boat with His disciples, the man who had been possessed begged Jesus to take him with them.

37. But Jesus did not let him, and said to him, "Go home to your people and report to them what great things the Lord has done for you and how He had mercy on you."

38. And the man went away and began to proclaim to the people what great things Jesus had done for him, and everyone was amazed.

CHAPTER 21

1. One day, as Jesus was traveling, two blind men followed Him, crying out "Have mercy on us!"

2. Jesus said to them, "Do you believe that I am able to do this?" They said to Him, "Yes, Lord."

3. Then He touched their eyes saying, "It shall be done for you according to your faith." And their eyes were opened, but Jesus sternly warned them to tell no one.

4. But they went out anyway and spread the news about Him throughout all the land.

5. And then a leader from among the people came to Jesus and said, "Teacher, I will follow You wherever You go. Show us the place where You are, for we must seek it."

6. But Jesus said to him, "The foxes have holes and the birds have nests, but the Son of Man has no where to lay His head."

7. One of those seeking to follow Him said, "I will follow You from here on out, but first let me go and bury my father. And Jesus said to him, "Let the dead bury the dead; you come and follow Me."

8. Another said, "I will follow You, Lord; but first permit me to say good-bye to those at home."

9. But Jesus said to him, "No one after setting his hand to the task and then looking back is fit for the kingdom of God."

10. Then the religious leaders came to Him and began to argue and demand a sign to test if He really was the Son of God.

11. But He answered them, "An evil and adulterous generation seeks for a sign; but no sign shall be given to it except the sign of the prophet Jonah. For as Jonah was three days and three nights in the belly of the whale, so will the Son of man be three days and three nights in the heart of the earth.

12. "The men of Nineveh will arise at the judgment with this generation and condemn it; for they repented at the preaching of Jonah, and behold, something greater than Jonah is here.

13. "The queen of the South will arise at the judgment with this generation and condemn it; for she came from the ends of the earth to hear the wisdom of Solomon, and behold, something greater than Solomon is here.

14. "Truly I tell you, an unclean spirit goes out of a man and passes through the abyss seeking rest and does not find it.

15. "So, it says to itself, 'I will return from where I came,' and when it arrives back it finds its old home unoccupied and

swept clean, and put in order. So it goes and takes along with it seven other spirits more wicked than itself, and they make their home there, and the last state of that person is worse than the first.

16. "And so it will be with this evil generation."

17. And turning to His disciples, He warned them, "beware of the leaven of the Pharisees and Sadducees."

18. But after He said this to them, they began to discuss among themselves that they had forgotten to get enough bread, and Jesus said to them, "Why are you discussing the fact that you have no bread?

19. "Do you not see or understand? Do you have a hardened heart already? Is it the case that having eyes, you do not see, and ears you do not hear?

20. "How many extra baskets did you fill when I fed the five thousand?"

21. And they answered Him, "twelve."

22. Then He said to them, "Do you not yet understand? Do not worry about bread; rather, be on guard against the bread the religious leaders and lawmakers prepare for you."

23. Soon after, they came to a village, and there they brought a blind man to Jesus and implored Him to heal him. So, Jesus took the blind man by the hand and led him out of the village.

24. Then He spat on the man's eyes and laid His hands on them and asked him, "Do you see anything?" The man replied, "I see people, but I see them like trees walking around."

25. So Jesus laid His hands on him again, and the man looked intently, and from then on began to see everything clearly.

26. Therefore, Jesus sent him home, saying, "Do not re-enter the village."

27. Then Jesus began to teach about those who claim to be religious saying, "A tree is known by the fruit that it bears; if the tree is bad, the fruit will be bad; if good, then the fruit will be good.

28. "You brood of vipers, how can you, being evil, speak of that which is good? For the abundance of the heart, the mouth speaks. The good person brings out of their treasure that which is good, and the evil bring from their treasure that which is evil.

29. "But I tell you that every careless word that people speak, they will give an account for it in the day of judgment. For by your words you will be justified, and by your words you will be condemned."

CHAPTER 22

1. Then Jesus began to teach His disciples saying, "Seek Me not because you saw signs, or because you ate of the loaves and were filled.

2. Do not work for food which wastes away, but work for the food which endures to eternal life, which the Son of Man will give you, for on Him God has set His seal."

3. So the disciples said to Him, "What should we do that we may do the works of God?"

4. Jesus answered, "This is the work of God, that you believe in Him whom He has sent.

5. "I am the bread of life; he who comes to Me will never hunger again. He who believes in Me will never thirst again."

6. Then they said to Him, "Lord always give us this bread."

7. And He answered, "But you have seen Me, and yet you still do not believe.

8. "All that the Father gives Me will come to Me, and the one who comes to Me, I will not cast out.

9. "For I have come down from heaven, not to do My will, but the will of Him who sent Me.

10. "For this is the will of the Father, that of all He has given Me, I will lose nothing, and that all who behold the Son and believe in Him will have eternal life, and I Myself will raise them up on the last day."

11. But then the religious leaders began grumbling about Him, because He said He was the bread of life.

12. They were saying to themselves, "Is this not the Jesus whose parents we know, whose father was a carpenter? And now He says He is the bread of life from heaven?"

13. But Jesus answered them saying, "Do not grumble among yourselves. No one can come to Me unless the Father who sent Me draws that person to Me; and it is that person whom I will raise up on the last day.

14. "Everyone who hears and learns from the Father comes to Me.

15. "Not that anyone has seen the Father, except the one who is from the Father; only that one has seen the Father.

16. "I say again, I am the bread of life; the life of the world is My flesh. He who eats My flesh and drinks My blood will live forever.

17. In truth, unless you eat the flesh of the Son of God and drink His blood, you have no life in you.

18. "Whoever drinks from My mouth will become like Me; I, Myself, shall become that person, and the hidden things will be revealed to them."

19. Then the people began to say, "How can this man give us His flesh to eat?"

20. But Jesus continued, "The one who eats My flesh and drinks My blood has eternal life in them, and I will raise them up on the last day.

21. "For My flesh is the true food, and My blood is the true drink, and the one who eats My flesh and drinks My blood abides in Me and I in them.

22. "Indeed, lucky is the lion that the human will eat, for then that beast becomes a human being.

23. "During the time when you ate what was dead, you made it alive with you. When you are in the light, what will you do?

24. "For just as the living Father sent Me, and I live because of the Father, so the one who eats of Me also lives, because of Me.

25. "On the day when you were one, you became two—but now you are two, so what is required?

26. "I am the bread of life. The one who eats this bread will live forever, and the living will never die."

27. These things Jesus taught in the temple; therefore, many of His disciples heard this teaching and said, "This is a hard teaching. Who can accept it?"

28. Jesus, conscious of what they were saying, said to them, "Does this cause you to stumble?

29. "Then what if you see the Son of Man ascending to where He was before?

30. "Truly I tell you, blessed is the one who does not take offense at Me."

31. "It is the spirit who gives life; the flesh counts for nothing; the words I have spoken to you are spirit, and they are life.

32. "But there are some of you who do not believe Me. For this reason, I have said to you that no one comes to Me unless the Father first grants it."

33. As a result of this teaching, many of His disciples fell away and no longer walked with Him. So Jesus asked the twelve disciples remaining, "Will you go away, too?"

34. But Peter answered Him, "Lord, to whom shall we go? You have the words of eternal life. We have believed and have come to know who You are—the Holy One of God."

35. Jesus answered them, "And yet one of you is Satan."

36. He said this meaning Judas, who would eventually betray Him. Yet each disciple wondered if they were the one.

CHAPTER 23

1. Jesus taught His disciples: "A student is not above the teacher, nor a slave above the master. It is enough for the student to become like the teacher, and it is enough that a slave become like the master.

2. "If they called the master Satan, how much more will they malign the members of the master's household? Truly I tell you, the one who receives you—receives Me.

3. "But do not fear them, for there is nothing concealed that will not be revealed or hidden that will not be known.

4. "What I tell you in the dark, speak in the light, and what you hear whispered in your ear, shout it from the housetops.

5. "Never fear those who can kill the body, but are unable to kill the soul; rather fear the one who can destroy both the body and the soul.

6. "Two foul are sold for a dollar, and yet not one falls to the ground apart from your Father.

7. "Indeed, even the very hairs of your head are numbered.

8. "So, never fear the world; you are far more valuable than many birds."

9. Then Jesus said, "I have cast fire upon the world, and I guard it until it blazes. How I wish it were already burning!

10. "But I have a baptism to undergo, and I am greatly distressed until it is finished.

11. "So, do not think that I have come to bring peace to the earth, for I did not come to bring peace, but a sword.

12. "I have come to cast conflicts upon the world—fire, sword, and wars!

13. "I came to set a man against his father, a daughter against her mother. Indeed, on account of Me, a person's enemies will be the members of their own household.

14. "For the one who does not hate their mother and father, sisters and brothers, husband or wife, and even their own life, is not worthy of Me. They cannot be My disciple.

15. "And the one who does not take up their cross daily and follow Me is not worthy of Me.

16. "For I tell you truly, the one who clings to their life will lose it, but the one who loses their life for My sake will find it.

17. "After all, which one of you, when you want to build a tower, does not first sit down and count the cost to see if you have enough to complete it?

18. "Otherwise, when you have laid the foundation and then are not able to finish, all who observe it will begin to ridicule you saying, 'You started a job but could not finish!'

19. "Or what king or queen, when setting out to battle another kingdom does not first sit down and consider if they are strong enough with ten thousand soldiers to encounter the enemy who has twenty thousand?

20. "If you do not give up all your possessions—if you do not give up your life, you cannot be My disciple."

CHAPTER 24

1. Then Thomas asked, "Lord what is the kingdom of God?"

2. Jesus spoke this parable to them, "To what shall I compare it? It is like a mustard seed that a person throws into their garden, and it grows into a tree, and the birds of the air nest in its branches.

3. "The kingdom of God is like yeast put into the dough; the dough is covered and hidden, and when it is seen again, it has grown many times its original size.

4. "The kingdom is like hidden treasure in a field, which the owner never knew was there. The owner died and left it to his children, but they never found the treasure themselves. When they died, a wanderer found the treasure. The wanderer hid the treasure again, and with much joy, sold all he had in order to buy the field and claim the treasure as his own.

5. "The kingdom is like a merchant seeking fine pearls, and upon finding one pearl of great value, the merchant goes and sells all that he has and buys that pearl.

6. "But the kingdom is also like a fisher's net cast into the sea gathering fish of every kind. But when the net is pulled up the good fish are gathered and the bad are thrown away.

7. "So it will be at the end of this age when the kingdom arrives: angels will come and take out the wicked from among the righteous and will throw them into the furnace of fire. In that place, there will be great weeping and gnashing of teeth.

8. "Have you understood what I have said to you?"

9. Thomas replied, "Yes, Lord I have understood it all."

10. And Jesus said to him, "Now you are like the head of a household who brings out of their treasure things new and old."

11. Soon after that, an argument started among the disciples as to who would be the greatest in the kingdom of God.

12. So, Jesus called a child over to Himself and set her before them and said to them, "Unless you are converted and become like children, you will not enter the kingdom of God.

13. "Whoever receives this child in My name receives Me, and whoever receives Me does not only receive Me, but receives Him who sent Me.

14. "Therefore, the one who is least among all of you is the one who will be the greatest in the kingdom, and the one who humbles themselves as a child is the one who will be first.

15. "Even more, whoever causes one such as this child who believes in Me to stumble, it would be better for that person to have a millstone hung about their neck and be cast into the depths of the sea.

16. "Truly I say to you, if you do not enter the kingdom of God like a child, you will never enter it at all. For the person old in years will ask a little child, seven days old, about the place in life, and that person will live.

17. "See that you do not despise one of these little ones, for I say to you that their angels in heaven continually see the face of My Father who is in heaven.

18. "For the first will be last, and all the last will become a single one.

19. "Who is greater? Is it the one who reclines at the table, or the one who serves at the table? Indeed it is the one who reclines. My Father has granted Me an everlasting kingdom, and yet I am among you as one who serves?

20. "But Just as My Father has granted Me a kingdom, I grant to you a kingdom, that you may always eat and drink at My table, and you will sit on thrones judging the twelve tribes of Israel.

21. "For you are the ones who have stood by Me in My trials.

22. "When you know yourselves, then you will understand that you are children of the Living Father. But if you do not know yourselves, then you live in poverty—indeed you have become that poverty."

23. Then He told a parable to some who trusted in themselves that they were righteous and viewed others with contempt, and He said:

24. "Two men went up to the church to pray to God, one a religious leader and the other a tax collector.

25. "The Pharisee stood and prayed: 'Thank You God that I am not like other people, the swindlers, the unjust, the adulterers, or even like this tax collector. I fast twice a week; I pay tithes of all that I get.'

26. "But the tax collector, standing some distance away, was even unwilling to lift up his eyes to heaven, but was beating his chest saying, 'God, be merciful, for I am a horrible sinner!'

27. "I tell you, the tax collector went to his house justified rather than the Pharisee. For everyone who exalts himself will be humbled, and the one who humbles himself will be exalted."

28. Then John said, "Master, we saw someone casting out demons in Your name; and we tried to prevent him, because he does not follow with us."

29. But Jesus said, "Do not hinder that one. For whoever is not against you is for you. And whoever performs miracles in My name will not speak bad of Me soon after."

30. As Jesus walked with His disciples they came to a town, but they were not permitted to enter it, because they were travelers, and James said to Jesus, "Lord, do You want us to call down fire and destruction from heaven to consume them?"

31. But Jesus turned to him and rebuked him, saying, "You do not know what spirit you are of; the Son of Man has come not to destroy lives, but to save them."

32. And they went on to another village, leaving that town to itself.

33. Some eight days later, Jesus took Peter, John and James up on a mountain, and there they began to pray, and as they did the face of Jesus became different and shone like the sun.

34. His clothing also changed and appeared white and gleaming like light, and behold, others were suddenly with Him and talking with Him about His departure from the world which would soon occur.

35. Peter said, "Lord, it is good for us to be here; if You wish, I will build temples for each of you."

36. But while Peter was speaking a cloud enveloped them all, and a voice out of the cloud said, "This is my beloved Son, in whom I am well pleased; listen to Him!"

37. When the disciples heard this they fell face down on the ground and were terrified.

38. But Jesus came to them and touched them and said, "Get up, and do not be afraid."

39. And lifting up their eyes, they saw no one except Jesus, Himself, alone.

40. As they were coming down from the mountain, Jesus commanded them to tell no one what they had seen until the Son of Man had been raised from the dead.

CHAPTER 25

1. One day, the Pharisees came to Jesus and said, "Why do Your disciples break the traditions of the elders? They do not even do ceremonial washings before they eat."

2. But He answered them, "And why do you transgress the commandment of God for the sake of your tradition?

3. For God commanded, 'Honor your father and your mother,' and, 'He who speaks evil of father or mother, let him surely die.'

4. But you say, 'If any one tells his father or his mother, What you would have gained from me is given to God, he need not honor his father.'

5. So, for the sake of your tradition, you have made void the word of God. You hypocrites! Well did Isaiah prophesy of you, when he said:

'This people honors me with their lips,

but their heart is far from me;

in vain do they worship me,

teaching as doctrines the precepts of men.'"

6. Then Jesus turned to His disciples and said, "Hear and understand: it is not what goes into the mouth that defiles a person, but rather what comes out of it that reveals the uncleanliness of a person."

7. The religious leaders then pressed Jesus, again asking for a sign to prove His authority to speak to them. They said to Him, "Tell us who You are, so that we may believe in You."

8. But He replied, "When it is evening, you say, 'It will be fair weather for the sky is red.' And in the morning you say, 'There will be a storm for the sky is red and it threatens us.'

9. "How is it that you can discern the weather from watching the sky, but you cannot discern the signs of the times?

10. "You examine the face of heaven and earth, but you have not come to know the one who is in your presence, and you do not know how to examine the present moment.

11. "An evil and adulterous generation seeks after a sign, and no sign will be given to it, except the Son of Man rising from the dead." And with that He left them and went away.

12. Then the disciples came to Him and said, "The Pharisees were greatly offended by what You said to them."

13. But Jesus said, "Every plant which My heavenly Father did not plant shall be uprooted.

14. "Let the Pharisees alone. They are blind guides leading the blind, and if a blind guide leads a blind person, both will fall into a pit."

15. Then Peter asked, "Jesus, explain the parable of 'eating' to us."

16. Jesus said, "Are you really lacking this understanding? Do you not know that everything that goes into the mouth passes into the stomach, and then is eliminated?

17. "But the things that come out of a person's mouth come from their heart, and it is that which is in the heart that defiles a person.

18. "For out of the heart comes all form of evil thoughts, murders, adulteries, fornications, thefts, lying and slander, covetousness, envy, pride, and foolishness.

19. "These are the things that defile a person, but to eat without ceremonial washing does no harm at all."

20. From there Jesus and His disciples came to a foreign town, and Jesus, trying not to be noticed, stayed in a house; but wherever He went the people soon found out.

21. Soon after, a woman from that region came to Him and began to cry out loudly, "Have mercy on me, Lord, for my daughter is cruelly possessed by a demon!"

22. But Jesus ignored her and went on His way, and His disciples came to Him and said, "Master, why do You not send her away for she continues to shout at us?"

23. He answered, "I was sent only to the lost sheep of the house of Israel."

24. But she came and began to bow down before Him, saying "Lord, help me, please."

25. Jesus said, "It is not right to take the children's food and give it to the dogs."

26. But the woman replied, "Yes, Lord, but even the dogs get to feed on the crumbs which fall from the children's table."

27. Then Jesus said to her, "O woman, your faith is great, and it shall be done for you as you wish," and her daughter was healed instantly.

28. While He was speaking to His disciples, someone came to Him and said, "Your mother and brothers are standing over there and wish to speak to You."

29. For they had come to take charge of Jesus, believing that He had lost his senses.

30. But Jesus answered saying, "Who is My mother, and who is my brother and sister?

31. "I tell you it is the one who does the will of My Father. Whosoever does the will of My Father is My mother and brother and sister, and they are the ones who will enter My Father's kingdom."

32. Then a woman said to Him, "Blessed is the womb that bore you!"

33. But He said to her, "Blessed are those who have heard the word of the Father and do it. For there will be days when you will say, 'Blessed are those who have never conceived.'"

34. When they came to Capernaum, the collectors of the half-shekel tax went up to Peter and said, "Does not your teacher pay the tax?"

35. And Peter replied, "Yes, He does!"

36. And when Peter came to Jesus about it, Jesus spoke to Him first saying, "What do you think, Peter: from whom do the kings of the earth collect taxes? Do they collect it from their children or from strangers?"

37. Peter replied, "They collect it from strangers."

38. "Then the children of the king are exempt. However, we do not want to offend them, so go to the sea and throw out a hook, and take the first fish you catch, and when you open it's mouth you will find two gold coins. Give it to the temple for you and for Me."

39. And Peter went fishing that very day and found everything as Jesus said he would.

CHAPTER 26

1. As they went through the region, a man was brought to Him who was deaf and spoke with great difficulty, and they implored Jesus to lay His hands on him.

2. So Jesus took him aside from the crowd, by himself, and put His fingers in the man's ears, and after spitting, He touched the spittle and then touched the man's tongue.

3. And looking up to heaven, with a deep sigh He said, "Be opened." And immediately the man could hear and began to speak plainly.

4. And Jesus gave them orders to tell no one of this miracle, but the more He ordered it, the more the people proclaimed it everywhere saying, "Who is this man? He has done all things well! He makes even the deaf to hear and the mute to speak!"

5. Then a man came to Jesus and fell before Him and begged, "Lord, have mercy on my son for he is a lunatic and is very ill. He often falls into the fire or into the water.

6. "I brought him to your disciples, but they could not cure him."

7. And Jesus asked him, "How long has he been this way?" And the father answered, "Since childhood. Please, if You can do anything, take pity on us and help him."

8. Jesus said to him, "If You can? All things are possible to those who believe."

9. And the father cried out, "I do believe, but help me with my disbelief!"

10. And Jesus turned to the crowd and said, "You unbelieving and perverted generation, how long will I be with you, How long shall I put up with you? Bring him here to Me."

11. And they brought the boy, and Jesus rebuked the demon, and it came out of him; and he was cured at once.

12. Then the disciples came to Jesus privately and said, "Why could we not drive it out?"

13. And He said to them, "Because of your little faith.

14. "Truly I tell you, if you have faith the size of a mustard seed, you will say to this mountain, 'Move from here to the sea,' and it will move and be cast into the sea.

15. "And when you make two into one—Behold, nothing shall be impossible to you.

16. "But this demon only comes out through much prayer and fasting."

17. And when He had gathered all the disciples together, He told them plainly. "I will not be with you much longer. The Son of Man will be delivered into the hands of men and they will kill Him. But He will rise again on the third day thereafter."

18. And the disciples were deeply grieved, and Mary wept openly at His feet.

19. Later, they returned to the town where Jesus had turned the water into wine, and a royal official heard of His return and went to Him, imploring Him to heal his son who was at the point of death.

20. Jesus said to him, "Unless you people see signs and wonders, you simply will not believe."

21. The nobleman said to Him, "Sir, come down now before my child dies."

22. And Jesus said, "Go, your son lives." So, the nobleman started off believing fully that Christ had healed his son.

23. As the nobleman approached his home, his workers came to him with joy saying that his son was now alive and well.

24. So, he inquired of them when he began to get better, and they said to him, "Yesterday around seven o'clock the fever left him." And the father knew that it was at that very time in which Jesus said to him, "Your son lives." And he, himself, along with his entire household believed in the Son of God.

25. After these things, Jesus stayed away from the cities, for in them the religious leaders were plotting to kill Him, and His time had not yet come.

CHAPTER 27

1. Then it came to pass that Jews' feast of tabernacles was at hand, and the brothers of Jesus came to Him saying, "Leave here, and go into the city so all Your followers may see the works You are doing.

2. "For no one does anything in secret when he himself seeks to be known publicly. If You really can do these things, then why not show Yourself to the world?"

3. His brothers said these things to Him, because even they were beginning to disbelieve in Him.

4. Nevertheless, Jesus stayed out of the city and told His brothers, "Go up to the feast yourselves; I do not go, because My time has not yet fully come."

5. But when His brothers had gone up to the feast, He then went Himself, but hidden rather than publicly.

6. When He got to the city, indeed the Jews were trying to find Him, asking, "Where is He?"

7. There was much grumbling in the crowds about Him; some were saying, "He is a good man." Others were saying, "No, He is the opposite, and He leads the people astray."

8. Yet no one would speak out for Him in public for fear of the Jews.

9. But as the feast was underway, Jesus revealed Himself in the temple and began to teach.

10. And the things He said astonished the Jews, and they said among themselves, "How has this man become learned having studied?"

11. So Jesus answered them and said, "My teaching is not Mine, but His who sent Me. If anyone is willing to do His will, that one will know whether this teaching is of God or whether I speak from Myself.

12. "Those who speak from themselves seek their own glory; but those who seek the glory of the Father who sent them, those are true, and there is no unrighteousness in them.

13. "Did not Moses give you the law you hold so dearly, and yet not one of you follows it. Why is it that you seek to kill Me?"

14. The crowd answered, "You have a demon! Who seeks to kill You?"

15. Jesus answered, "From the time I healed a man on the Sabbath, you have sought to kill Me. But you would have been better to judge with righteous judgment."

16. Some of the people in the crowed were asking, "Is this not the man the Jews are seeking to arrest? But look; He is speaking publicly and they are saying nothing to Him. They must not know that He is the Christ."

17. And some in the crowd said, "This cannot be the Christ, because we know where this man is from. When the Christ comes, no one will know where He is from."

18. Jesus, hearing this, cried out in the temple, "You know Me, and you know where I am from, but you do not know the one who sent Me. I know the one who sent Me, because I am from Him."

19. In saying these things, Jesus angered the crowd, and they sought to capture Him and execute Him, but no one laid a hand on Him, because His time had not yet come.

20. Still, many in the crowd came to believe in Jesus, because they said to themselves, it would not be possible for Christ to come and do more signs than He has done.

21. The Pharisees heard the crowd muttering these things about Jesus, so the chief priests sent out officers to seize Him.

22. Knowing this, Jesus said to the people, "For a little while longer I am with you, then I go to Him who sent Me.

23. "Often you have longed to hear these things from Me, and you have no one else from whom to hear them. Yet soon, you will look for Me, but you will not find Me; for where I am you cannot come."

24. And the people said, "Where is this man going that we will not find Him?"

25. Then on the last day of the feast, Jesus cried out, "If anyone is thirsty, let that one come to Me and drink, and anyone who believes in Me, from their innermost being will flow rivers of living water!"

26. Even the officers of the chief priests returned to the leaders saying, "Never has a man spoke like this."

27. But the Pharisees mocked them saying, "Have you also been fooled and led astray!"

28. Nicodemus (the one who spoke with Jesus in the night) said, "Surely we are not going to condemn a man before hearing what He has to say?"

29. But they answered him, "Look in our scriptures and you will see that Christ does not come from us."

30. And then each of them went their own way to their own homes.

31. But Jesus, Himself, went to the Mount of Olives.

CHAPTER 28

1. Early in the morning Jesus came back to the temple, and all the people were coming to Him, and He sat down to teach them.

2. The scribes and Pharisees, wanting to test Him, brought before Him a woman caught in adultery and set her in the center of the court before Him.

3. They said to Him, "Teacher, our law says she must be stoned to death for her sins; what do you say?"

4. But Jesus said nothing and with His finger began to write in the dust.

5. But they persisted in asking Him, so that they might have grounds for accusing Him. But again, He only wrote in the dirt.

6. When they asked him a third time, He stood up and said, "Let the one who is without sin be the first to cast a stone."

7. But when the religious leaders heard this, they began to go out of the court one by one, beginning with the older ones, until eventually the woman was left alone with Jesus.

8. Jesus asked her, "Where are your accusers. Does not anyone condemn you?"

9. The woman answered, "No one, my Lord."

10. And Jesus said to her, "Neither do I condemn you. Go and sin no more."

11. Thereafter, the chief religious leaders convened a council and were saying, "This man, Jesus, is performing many miracles, and we are doing nothing. If we let Him go on, all the people will believe in Him, and the government will come and take away our place."

12. Then the chief priest, Caiaphas, said to them, "Do you not realize it is better for one man to die than for an entire nation to perish?"

13. But Caiaphas did not say this on his own accord, but being high priest that year, he prophesied that Jesus should die for the nation..

14. So from that day forward, they planned together to kill Jesus; and for that reason, Jesus no longer walked publicly among the Jews or the temple. Instead He went to a small town in the countryside where He stayed with His disciples only.

15. And the chief priest and the Pharisees gave orders that anyone knowing the whereabouts of Jesus must report it so that He might be seized.

16. Now, in the small town a crowd had gathered to hear Jesus teach. And in the crowd two blind men hearing the voice of Jesus cried out, "Lord have mercy on us!"

17. But the others in the crowd told them to be silent, but that only made the blind men cry out more.

18. So Jesus called to them and said, "What do you want Me to do for you?"

19. They said to Him, "Lord we want our eyes opened."

20. Moved with compassion for the blind men, Jesus touched their eyes and they began immediately to see, and they followed Jesus from then on.

CHAPTER 29

1. Then Jesus began to teach His disciples saying, "Woe to the world because of its stumbling blocks. Such stumbling blocks must come, but woe to the one through whom they come.

2. "If your hand or foot causes you to stumble, cut it off and throw it from you; it is better to enter life crippled or lame, than to have two hands or two feet and be cast into hell.

3. "If your eye causes you to stumble, pluck it out and throw it away from you. It is better for you to enter life with one eye, than to have two eyes and be cast into the fires of hell.

4. "For it is not the will of your Father who is in heaven that even one of his children should perish."

5. Then Peter asked, "Lord, how many times shall I forgive my neighbor if he sins against me? Seven times?"

6. Jesus said to him, "Not seven times, but seventy times seven.

7. "For this reason, the kingdom of God may be compared to a king who wished to settle accounts with his servants.

8. "As he began to settle their accounts, one was brought to him who owed ten thousand talents, but the servant did not have the means to pay, so his lord commanded him to be sold as a slave, along with his wife and children, and all that he had in order to make the repayment.

9. "But the servant fell to the ground and begged his lord saying, 'Please lord, give me just a little more time, and I will repay everything to you.'

10. "And the lord felt compassion for his servant and released him, while at the same time forgiving all his debt.

11. "But the servant went out and found one who was a servant to him and owed him money, and he seized him and began to assault him, saying, 'Payback everything you owe me.'

12. "So his fellow servant fell to his knees and begged him saying, 'Have patience with me, and I will repay everything.'

13. "But the servant was unwilling and had him thrown in prison until he could pay back what was owed to him.

14. "Deeply grieved, the other servants went to the lord and told him everything that had happened. And the lord re-summoned his servant.

15. "And he said to him, 'You wicked servant, I forgave you all that debt because you pleaded with me. Why did you not have mercy on those who owed you money, just as I had with you?'

16. "And his lord, moved with anger, handed him over to the torturers until he repaid all that was owed to him.

17. "Your heavenly Father will do the same with you, if each of you does not forgive your brother or sister from your heart."

18. Then some Pharisees came to Jesus and tested Him by asking, "Is it lawful for a man to divorce his wife for any reason at all?"

19. And He answered them saying, "Have you not learned that God, from the beginning, created them male and female and said, 'For this reason a man will leave his father and mother and be joined to his wife, and the two of them shall become one flesh'?

20. "So they are no longer two but one, and what God has joined together, let no one tear asunder.

21. "Divorce was never intended from the beginning, and therefore anyone who divorces their spouse, except for infidelity, and then marries another, is committing adultery."

22. So His disciples said to Him, "If marriage is like this, perhaps a person should never marry."

23. And Jesus said, "Not everyone can accept this, but only those to whom it has been given.

CHAPTER 30

1. Then His disciples asked Him about the Kingdom of God, and Jesus said to them, "The Kingdom of God is like a landowner who went out early in the morning to hire laborers for his vineyard.

2. "When he agreed with the workers on a certain daily wage, he sent them into the vineyard, and then he went out about three o'clock and saw others standing idle in the market place.

3. "To those he said, 'You also go into my vineyard, and whatever is right I will pay you.' And so they, too, went into the vineyard.

4. "Again he went out toward the end of the day, and did the same thing. Finding even more, he said to them, 'why have you been standing around all day long?'

5. "They said to him, 'Because no one has put us to work.' So, he said to them, 'You may go work in the vineyard, too.'

6. "When the night came, the owner of the vineyard said to the foreman, 'Call the laborers and pay them their wages, beginning with the last hired and work toward the first.'

7. "When those hired at the end of the day came, they were paid the day's wage. When those hired first came, they thought they would receive more, but instead they were paid the daily wage agreed upon.

8. "When the first hired received their wage they grumbled about the vineyard owner saying, 'These last men have worked only one hour and you have made them equal to us who have suffered the work and the heat all day.'

9. "But the owner answered them saying, 'I have not wronged you; did you not agree on the wages you were paid? Take your wage and leave, but I want to give these last workers the same as you. Is it not within my rights to do with my money what I wish, or are you angry because I am generous?'

10. "So shall the first be last and the last be first."

11. After this, Jesus took his twelve disciples to another place and reminded them, "We are soon to return to Jerusalem where the Son of Man must be delivered to the elders and chief priests and scribes, and they will condemn him to death, and deliver him to the Gentiles to be mocked and scourged and crucified, and he will be raised on the third day."

12. Later, the mother of two of Jesus' disciples, James and John, came to Him with her sons and said, "Lord, command that in Your kingdom these two sons of mine may sit one on Your right and the other on Your left."

13. But Jesus answered her and said, "You do not know what you are asking for. Are you able to drink from the cup that I am about to drink? Can you be baptized with My baptism?"

14. The two said to Him, "We can."

15. Then Jesus said, "Indeed My cup you will drink from, and with My baptism you will be baptized, but to sit at the right hand and the left is not Mine to give you. It is for those whom it has been prepared for by My Father."

16. Hearing this request the ten others became indignant with the two brothers, but Jesus called them all together and said, "You know that the rulers of the people of the world lord it over them, and their rulers lord it over them, but it is not that way with you.

17. "Whoever wishes to become great among you, must be the servant of you, and whoever wishes to be first among you must be like your slave.

18. "Just as the Son of God did not come to be served, but to serve and to give His life as a ransom for many."

19. After this, He went to another town, and His disciples were going along with Him, and a large crowd followed after them.

20. As He approached the town gate, a dead man was being carried out. The man was the only son of his mother, and she was also a widow, and a large crowd accompanied her in her sorrow.

21. When the Lord saw her, He felt compassion for her and said, "Do not weep, mother," and He went to the coffin and stopped the bearers and said to the dead young man, "Arise."

22. Immediately the dead man sat up and began to speak, and Jesus gave him back to his mother.

23. When they witnessed this, fear gripped the crowd and they said, "A great prophet has arisen among us. God has visited His people!"

24. So it was that this report concerning Him went out over all the surrounding districts.

CHAPTER 31

1. There came a time when one of the Pharisees, Simon, was requesting that Jesus dine with him and his colleagues in secret. So Jesus came to Simon's house and entered it, and sat at the table.

2. Also there was a prostitute in this same village. When she heard that Jesus was sitting at the table in the religious leader's house, she brought to the house an alabaster jar of perfumed lotion.

3. And standing behind Him, she fell to her knees weeping and began to wet His feet with her tears. She wiped the tears off His feet with her hair and anointed them with the perfume.

4. When Simon saw this, he said to himself, "If this man were a prophet, He would know who and what sort of person this woman is who is touching Him, for she is a sinner."

5. And Jesus answered him, "Simon, I have something to say to you."

6. And Simon answered asking, "What is it, Teacher."

7. "A money lender had two debtors: one owed five hundred and the other owed fifty.

8. "When they were unable to pay their debt, he forgave them both. So, which of them will love him more?"

9. Simon answered, "I suppose the one that received the most forgiveness." And Jesus said to him, "You have judged correctly."

10. Turning to the woman, Jesus said to Simon, "Do you see this woman? I entered your house, but you gave Me no water to wash My feet, and yet she has washed them with her tears and dried them with her hair.

11. "You did not welcome Me with so much as a handshake, but she has not stopped kissing My feet since I arrived.

12. "For this reason I say to you, her sins, which are many, have been forgiven, for she has loved much; but the one who is self-righteous loves little."

13. Then He said to her, "Your sins are forgiven."

14. But the others at the table with Him began to say to themselves, "Who is this man that He dare to forgive sins?"

15. And He said to the woman, "Go in peace; your faith has saved you."

16. At that point a lawyer stood up at the table and wanting to put Jesus to the test asked Him, "Teacher, what should I do to inherit eternal life?"

17. Jesus replied, "What is written in the law? How do you interpret it?"

18. And the lawyer replied, "You should love God with all your heart, all your mind, all your soul, and all your strength; and you should love your neighbor as yourself."

19. Jesus said to him, "You have answered correctly. Do this, and you will live."

20. But wishing to complicate the matter, he asked, "But who is my neighbor?"

21. Jesus replied, "A man was going down from Jerusalem to Jericho and fell among robbers on the road. They stripped him, beat him, and went away leaving him nearly dead.

22. "By chance a priest was going down that road, and when he saw him, he passed by on the other side.

23. "Likewise a Levite also came by, but when he came to the place where the man lay and saw him, he too crossed and passed him by.

24. "But a Samaritan, as he journeyed, came to where he was; and when he saw him, he felt compassion for him.

25. "He medicated and bandaged the man's wounds, put him on his own beast and brought him to an inn where he was well known and took care of him through the night, watching that he did not worsen.

26. "In the morning, he gave the innkeeper money, and said, 'Take care of him, and whatever money you spend, when I return, I will repay you.'

27. "Now, which of these three do you think proved to be a neighbor to the man who fell into the robber's hands?"

28. And the lawyer answered, "The one who showed mercy toward him."

29. Jesus replied, "Go and do likewise."

CHAPTER 32

1. Before they ate, a Pharisee noticed that Jesus did not take part in their ceremonial washing before sitting at the table, and he was shocked by it.

2. But Jesus said, "See how you Pharisees carefully wash the outside of the cup, but you leave the inside full of robbery and wickedness.

3. "You foolish people: Did not the one who made the outside make the inside as well?

4. "Rather you should clean the inside of the cup and alms from that which is within. Then all things will be clean for you.

5. "But woe to you religious leaders; for you offer to God a tenth of your wealth, and then neglect the very justice and love of God. You would do better to use the former for the latter.

6. "Woe to you religious leaders, for you love to sit in the chief seats of the Church and be recognized with honor in the marketplace.

7. "So I tell you that when you fast, you bring sin upon yourselves; and if you pray, you will be condemned; and if you give to charity, you will damage your soul.

8. "Woe to you religious leaders for you are like unmarked graves which people walk over unaware. You are like whitewashed tombs: clean on the outside but full of death."

9. Then one of the religious leaders stood and said, "When You say these things, You insult all of us!"

10. But Jesus replied, "You insult yourselves; for you weigh men down with heavy burdens, while you would never touch the burdens with one of your fingers.

11. "Woe to you, for you build tombs for the righteous heroes and prophets and then honor them after killing them.

12. "For this reason the wisdom of God has said, 'I will send them prophets and apostles, and they will persecute and kill them, and then shall it be that all the blood of the prophets and apostles shall be charged against this generation.'

13. "Woe to you scribes and Pharisees, for you are like dogs sleeping in the cattle manger: The dogs do not eat, neither do they let the cattle eat.

14. "You have taken away the keys of knowledge. You do not enter the kingdom of God, nor do you allow those who want to enter to do so."

15. When Jesus left there, the religious leaders became very hostile towards Him, and whenever they questioned Him, they questioned Him closely, plotting to trap Him in His own words.

16. Later a crowd formed around Jesus and His disciples in order to hear His teachings. From the crowd someone said to Him, "Teacher, tell my brother to divide the family inheritance with me."

17. But Jesus said, "Who appointed Me a judge or arbitrator over you?" And He turned to His disciples and asked, "I am not a divider of property, am I?"

18. Then He taught saying, "Be on your guard against every form of greed, for even when one has abundance, their life does not consist of their possessions."

19. And He told them a parable, saying, "The land of a rich man yielded a great harvest, and he began to reason with himself saying, 'What shall I do, since I have nowhere to store all my crops?'

20. "Then he said, 'I know what I will do. I will tear down my old barns and build new larger barns and I will store up all my harvest and my wealth. Then I can say to myself, soul, you have many goods laid up for many years. Take your ease from here on out; eat, drink and be merry.'

21. "But God said to him, 'You fool! This night your soul is required of you; and now who will own what you have prepared?'

22. "And so it is with the people who store up treasures from themselves rather than treasures from God.

23. "Sell your possessions and give the money out of compassion to others, and make money belts that do not wear out.

24. Make for yourself an unfailing treasure in heaven where no thief steals it away and no decay destroys it.

25. For wherever your treasure is, there too is your heart.

26. "Do not be afraid My chosen ones, for the Father gladly gives you His kingdom.

27. "Therefore, let the one who has become wealthy reign, and the one who has power renounce it."

28. Now, there were some present who reported to Jesus about the Galileans, whose blood Pilate had mingled with their sacrifices.

29. And Jesus said to them, "Do you suppose that these Galileans were greater sinners than all others and this is why they suffered their fate?

30. "I tell you, no, but unless you repent, you will all likewise perish.

31. "Or do you suppose that the eighteen who were killed when the tower in Siloam fell were worse sinners than all the others who dwelt in Jerusalem?

32. "I tell you, no, but unless you repent, you will likewise die."

33. And then He told a parable, "A man had a fig tree which had been planted in his vineyard, and he came looking for fruit on it, but did not find any.

34. "So, he said to the gardener of the vineyard, 'Behold, three years I have come looking for fruit on this tree without finding any. Cut it down! Why does it even use up the soil?

35. "But the gardener answered him saying, 'Let it alone this year as well, and I will dig around it and put in fertilizer; if it bears fruit next year, fine, but if not we shall cut it down.'"

CHAPTER 33

1. Then Jesus said, "Be on guard against the world, prepare yourselves with great strength, so robbers cannot find a way to get you, for the trouble you expect will come."

2. "Truly, I tell you, if the head of the house had known what hour the thief was coming, he would not have let his house be broken into.

3. "Therefore, be dressed in readiness with your lamps lit, for as well the Son of Man is coming at an hour you do not know.

4. Later, He was teaching in a church on the sabbath, and a woman came to Him who for eighteen years had been sickened by a spirit, and because of this she was bent over and could not stand up straight.

5. When Jesus saw her, He called her to Him and said, "Woman, you are freed from your sickness."

6. And He laid His hands on her, and she immediately stood up straight and began to glorify God.

7. But the Pharisees were angered and offended that He had again performed healings on the sabbath, and they began saying to the crowd in response: "There are six days to work—so why do you not come on those days to be healed?"

8. But Jesus said to them, "You hypocrites! Do not each of you on the sabbath feed and water your animals, yet this woman—one of your own and one of God's own, whom Satan has afflicted all these years—should she not be released from this bond on the sabbath?

9. "If you do not observe the sabbath as a sabbath, you will never see the Father."

10. And as Jesus said these things to them, they became humiliated, and the entire crowd was rejoicing over the glorious things being done by Him.

11. And He was passing from one village and town to the next, teaching as He went, and proceeding on His way to Jerusalem.

12. And Mary asked Him, "Lord, is everybody to be saved or only a few?"

13. And Jesus said, "The Father chooses one from a thousand and two from ten thousand and they stand together as a single one.

14. "If you bring forth what is within you, what you have will save you. If you do not have that within you, what you do not have within you will kill you."

15. Just at that time, some Pharisees ran up to Him and said, "You must flee now. Herod is looking to kill you."

16. And Jesus said to them, "Go tell that fox that today I cast out demons and perform cures, and tomorrow I do the same, and on the third day I reach my goal.

17. "But, nevertheless, I must move on today, and journey the next day, and the next, for my time is coming, and it cannot be that a prophet should perish anywhere but in Jerusalem.

18. "O Jerusalem, the city that kills its prophets and stones those sent to her. How often I have wanted to gather your children together, just as a hen gathers her brood under her wings, but you would not have it!

19. "In the past, I did not tell you the things about which you asked Me. Now, I am willing to tell them to you, but you are not seeking them.

20. "Behold, your house is on fire; and truly I tell you, you will not see Me until the day when you say, 'Blessed is the one who comes in the name of the Lord.'"

21. Then Jesus taught His disciples saying, "When you are invited by someone to a feast, do not take the place of honor as if it were owed to you, for it could be that someone more important will come and you will be asked to move for that person. Then all will see your shame.

22. "But when you come to the table, take the lowest place, and then when you are invited to sit at a higher seat, your honor will be shown to all.

23. "For everyone who exalts themselves will be humbled, and everyone who humbles themselves will be exalted.

24. "And when you give, give to those who cannot return the favor, lest they do return the favor and you are paid in full before receiving your reward in the kingdom of heaven."

25. Then He said to them, "A woman was holding a banquet and invited many people to come, and at the dinner hour, she sent her servant to say to those who had been invited, 'Come now, for everything has been prepared.'

26. "But they all began to make excuses. One said to the servant, 'I have bought some land, and I need to go look at it; please ask her to excuse my absence.'

27. "The next said, 'I have bought many horses, and I need to go see how they run. Thank her for the offer and tell her I cannot come.'

28. "The third said, 'I have just been married, so I will not be there.'

29. "When the servant came back to the woman and reported all this, she became angry and ordered the servant to the streets to call in the poor, sick, lame, and blind to dine with her.

30. "And when her house was full, she said to her servant, 'Those first invited shall never dine in my house again.'"

CHAPTER 34

1. Now all the tax collectors and sinners were coming to listen to Jesus speak, and the religious leaders began to grumble saying, "This man receives sinners and eats with them!"

2. So Jesus related a parable to them saying, "What man among you if he had a hundred sheep and one had gone astray, would not leave the ninety-nine in the open pasture on the hillsides and go into the valley to search for the one that was lost?

3. "When he finds the sheep, he is overjoyed, and tells all his friends that he has finally found his lost sheep. And to that sheep he says, 'I love you more than the ninety-nine.'

4. "I tell you that in the same way there will be more joy in heaven over one sinner who repents than over ninety-nine righteous persons who need no repentance.

5. "Or what woman, if she has ten gold coins, and loses one, does not light all her lamps and search the house carefully until she finds it? When she finds it, she calls together her friends and neighbors saying, 'Rejoice with me, for I have found my gold coin which was lost!'

6. "In the same way, I tell you there is joy in the presence of the angels of God over one sinner who repents."

7. Then Jesus gave this parable, "A man had two sons. The younger one said to his father, 'Father, give me the share of the inheritance that is mine.' So, he divided his wealth between his two sons.

8. "Not long after, the younger son gathered his possessions and went on a journey to a distant country, and there he wasted his entire estate on loose living.

9. "After he had spent all his wealth, a severe famine occurred in that country, and he began to starve.

10. "So, he begged for a job from one of the citizens of that country and they sent him to work feeding the pigs. But the wages were nearly nothing, and even the swine were eating better then he.

11. "One day, while working, he realized, 'My father's workers have more than enough to eat while I am dying here with hunger.

12. 'I will go to my father and say to him: Father, I have sinned against heaven and in your sight, I am no longer worthy to be called your son, but make me as one of your hired men, and that will be enough.'

13. "So, he got up and journeyed back to his father. But while he was still a long way off, his father spotted him and felt love for him, and ran up and embraced him.

14. "And the son said to his father, 'Father, I have sinned against you, I am no longer worthy to be called your son.'

15. "But his father shouted to his servants, 'Quickly, bring out the best robe and put it on him. Put a ring on his finger and good shoes on his feet, and bring out the best meat to cook; for tonight we are having a great feast and celebration!

16. 'For this child of mine was dead and has come to life again; he was lost and now is found!' And they began to celebrate.

17. "Now, his older son was in the fields, and when he approached the house, he heard music and dancing.

18. "And a servant said to him, 'Your brother has come home and your father has made a feast and a celebration, because he has received him back safe and sound.'

19. "But the older son was angry and refused to go in and join the celebration. So, his father came out and pleaded with him to come in.

20. "The older son answered his father, 'For many years I have been serving you and never ignored one of your commands, and yet you have never given me anything so that I might have a celebration with my friends.

21. 'But when this child of yours comes home, who has devoured your wealth with prostitutes and wine, you have a great celebration.'

22. "The father said, 'This is true, but you have been with me always, and all that is mine has always been yours; we have to celebrate and rejoice, for this brother of yours was dead and has begun to live; he was lost, but now he is found.'"

23. Then Jesus said to them, "What do you think? A man had two sons, and he came to the first and said 'Son, go work in the vineyard today,' and the son rebelled saying, 'I will not!' But later he felt guilty and went and worked in the vineyard.

24. "The other son said, 'I will go and work in the vineyard,' but then did not ever go. Which one did the will of the father?"

25. The disciples answered, "The first."

26. And Jesus said, "The kingdom of God will be filled with such."

CHAPTER 35

1. Now, Jesus also taught His disciples saying, "There was a rich man who had a manager, and this manager was reported to him for squandering the rich man's wealth.

2. "So, he called in the manager one day and said to him 'What is this I hear about you? You must give a final account of your management of my wealth, and then you can no longer be my manager.'

3. "The manager said to himself, 'What shall I do now that I am losing my position as a manager? I am too proud to beg, and I am not strong enough for manual labor.'

4. 'I know what I will do, so that when I am removed from my job, I will still have many favors to call in.'

5. "And he summoned each one of his master's debtors, and he began saying to the first, 'How much do you owe my master?'

6. "And he said, 'A hundred measures of oil.'

7. "So the manager said, 'Take your bill, and sit down and quickly write it for fifty.'

8. "Then he said to another, 'How much do you owe?' And she said, 'I owe a hundred measures of wheat'; so, he said to her, 'Take your bill and make it out for eighty.'

9. "And to his surprise, the wealthy master praised his un-righteous manager, because he acted shrewdly; for the children of this age are more shrewd in relation to their own kind than are the sons and daughters of the Light.

10. "So I say to you, make friends for yourselves by means of unrighteous wealth, so that when it fails, they will receive you into their eternal dwellings.

11. "The one who is faithful in a very little thing is faithful also in much; and the one who is unrighteous in a very little thing is also unrighteous in much.

12. "Therefore, if you have not been faithful in the use of un-righteous wealth, who will entrust the true riches to you?

13. "And if you have not been faithful in the use of that which is another's, who will give you that which is your own?

14. "From everyone who has been given much will much be required, and to the one who has been entrusted with much, all the more shall be required.

15. "A person cannot mount two horses or bend two bows. No servant can serve two masters; for either they will hate the one and love the other, or else they will be devoted to one and despise the other. You cannot serve God and money."

16. Now the Pharisees, who were lovers of money, were listening in and scoffing at Him.

17. And He said to them, "You are those who justify yourselves in the sight of men, but God knows your hearts; for that which is highly esteemed among men is detestable in the sight of God."

18. Then Jesus said, "There was a rich man, who was clothed in purple and fine linen and who feasted sumptuously every day.

19. "And at his gate lay a poor man named Lazarus, full of sores, who desired to be fed with what fell from the rich man's table; moreover the dogs came and licked his sores.

20. "The poor man died and was carried by the angels to Abraham's bosom.

21. "The rich man also died and was buried, and in Hades, being in torment, he lifted up his eyes, and saw Abraham far off and Lazarus in his bosom.

22. "And he called out, 'Father Abraham, have mercy upon me, and send Lazarus to dip the end of his finger in water and cool my tongue; for I am in anguish in this flame.'

23. "But Abraham said, 'Son, remember that you in your lifetime received your good things, and Lazarus in like manner evil things; but now he is comforted here, and you are in anguish.

24. "And besides all this, between us and you a great chasm has been fixed, in order that those who would pass from here to you may not be able, and none may cross from there to us.'

25. "And he said, 'Then I beg you, father, to send him to my father's house, for I have five brothers, so that he may warn them, lest they also come into this place of torment.'

26. "But Abraham said, 'They have Moses and the prophets; let them hear them.'

27. "And he said, 'No, father Abraham; but if some one goes to them from the dead, they will repent.'

28. "He said to him, 'If they do not hear Moses and the prophets, neither will they be convinced if some one should rise from the dead.'"

29. Then Phillip said to Jesus, "Lord increase our faith."

30. And Jesus said to him, "If you had faith the size of a mustard seed, you would say to the oak tree, 'Be uprooted and cast into the lake,' and it would obey you."

31. Then as they were walking, ten lepers stood at a distance and shouted to Christ to heal them saying, "Master, have mercy on us!"

32. When He saw them, He said, "Go show yourselves to the priests and Pharisees. And as they went, they were healed along the way."

33. And one of them, a foreigner, turned back and began to glorify God with a loud voice, falling at Jesus' feet and thanking Him.

34. And Jesus said, "Were not ten cured? But the other nine, where are they? Only this one foreigner has glorified God for his miracle."

35. So, He said to him, "Go now, for it is your faith that has made you well."

CHAPTER 36

1. While they were listening, Jesus went on to tell a parable, because His disciples were anticipating the arrival of the kingdom of God.

2. He said to them, "A nobleman went to a distant country to receive a kingdom for himself, and then to return.

3. "So, he called ten of his servants and gave them all ten gold coins to use in business until he returned.

4. "But some of the servants hated him and sent a delegation after him saying, 'We do not want you to reign over us.'

5. "When the nobleman returned as a king, he ordered his servants to whom he had given money to be called to him so that he might take account of what they had done.

6. "The first came to him and said, 'I have taken your gold coins and made ten more with them.'

7. "And he said to him, 'Well done, my good and faithful servant, you have been faithful in a little thing, so I will make you ruler of ten cities.'

8. "The second servant came to him and said, 'I took your ten gold coins and made five more.'

9. "And he said to him also, 'Well done; I will give you the rule of five cities.'

10. "But another servant came to him and said, 'Master, here is your ten gold coins, which I have kept in a safe place so that I may return them to you. For I was afraid of you, because you are an exacting man. You reap what you did not sow, and you take up what you have not laid down.'

11. "So, the king said to him, 'By your own words shall you be judged, you worthless servant.

12. 'If you knew that I was an exacting man, reaping what I did not sow, and pulling up what I did not lay down, why did you not at least put my money in a bank where it could earn interest?'

13. "Then he said so all could hear, 'Take the gold coins from him and give it to the one who has ten.'

14. "But some said to him, 'Master, he has ten already.'

15. "And he said to them, 'I tell you that to the one who has will more be given, and to the one who has not, even what he thinks he has shall be stripped from him.

16. 'Take this lazy one out and cast him into the outer darkness where there is weeping and gnashing of teeth.

17. 'And as for those who sent the delegation to tell me not to return, bring them to me and slay them in front of me.'"

18. Then He told them a parable to show that at all times they ought to pray and not lose heart.

19. And He said, "In a certain city there was a judge who did not fear God and did not respect man.

20. "There was a widow in that city who came to him continually asking that he grant her justice against her adversary.

21. "For a while, he was unwilling to do so, but later he said to himself, 'Though I fear neither God nor respect man, still I will give her what she wants or she will wear me out.'

22. "Listen to what the unrighteous judge has said. And will not God bring justice for His elect who cry out to Him day and night, or will He delay?

23. "I tell you that the Father will bring about justice for His elect quickly.

24. "But when the Son of Man comes, will he find faith on the earth?"

25. Then Jesus and His disciples were passing through a town on the way to the Holy City, and there was a man named Zaccheus. He was the chief tax collector and was very rich.

26. Zaccheus was trying to see who Jesus was, and was unable to because of the crowd, for he was a short man.

27. So, he ran ahead and climbed a sycamore tree in order to see Him, for Jesus was about to pass that way.

28. When Jesus came to the place, He looked up and said to him, "Zaccheus, come down from that tree, for tonight I am staying at your house."

29. So, Zaccheus climbed down hurriedly and received Him gladly.

30. But when the crowd saw all this, they grumbled, saying, "He has gone to be the guest of a man who is a great sinner."

31. Zaccheus stopped and said to the Lord, "Behold Lord, I will give half of all my possessions to the poor, and if I have defrauded anyone of anything, I will give it all back—four times as much!"

32. And Jesus said to him, "Today salvation has come to this house, because you, too, are a son of Abraham.

33. "For the Son of Man has come to save that which was lost."

CHAPTER 37

1. One day, Jesus and His disciples were walking by the temple, and Peter pointed out to Him, "Teacher, behold what wonderful stonework has made this magnificent building."

2. And Jesus said to them, "Do you see these great buildings? I tell you truly, not one stone will be left upon another that will not be thrown down."

3. Then they all went to the top of a hill that overlooked Jerusalem, and Peter, James, John and Andrew came to Him asking, "When will these things happen, and what will be the sign of the end of the age when Your kingdom comes into being?"

4. And Jesus said to them, "See that no one deceives you. For the kingdom of God will not come with signs and wonders, nor will it come by watching for it.

5. "Behold, the kingdom of God is within you, and it is among you, and it is spread out upon the earth, but people do not see it.

6. "And a time is coming when you will long to see even one day of the Son of Man, but you will not be able to see it.

7. "And many will come in that day and say, 'Look in the desert, or look in the city—Christ has returned!' but do not believe it.

8. "For wherever the carcass is, there will the vultures gather.

9. "And many will come in My name saying, 'I am the Christ, follow Me.' And they will perform signs and wonders that would deceive even the very elect if that were possible. For behold, I have told you everything in advance.

10. "For just as lightning is visible in the whole sky, so will be the coming of the Son of Man in His day.

11. "You will hear of wars and rumors of wars, but see that you are not frightened, because that is not the end.

12. "For always nation will rise against nation, and one kingdom will replace another, and there will be famines and earthquakes in various places, but all these things are only the beginning of birth pains.

13. "For first the Son of Man must suffer many things and be rejected by this generation.

14. "Then the end will come suddenly when no one expects it. People will be eating and drinking, and buying and selling, and marrying and planting, and building.

15. "Many false prophets will arise and deceive many, and because lawlessness will abound, the love of many will become cold, but those who endure to the end will be saved.

16. "You will be hated by all nations because of me, and they will persecute you and kill you and deliver you up to be tried. You will be thrown out of the synagogues and beaten, and forced to give account of yourselves.

17. "But do not worry beforehand what you will say, for the Holy Spirit will give you the words to speak.

18. "Brother will betray brother, and a father will betray his child, and the children will rise up against their parents and have them put to death.

19. "When you see the abomination that causes desolation standing where it should not be, then flee to the wilderness, and do not go back for your possessions. Do not even go back for your coat.

20. "How sad it will be in that day for women who are pregnant and those with small children. So pray, therefore, that your flight does not take place in the winter.

21. "For those days will be a time of tribulation such as the world has never seen and will never see again.

22. "Unless the Father shortens those days, no life will be left, but He will shorten those days for the sake of the elect whom He has chosen.

23. "I tell you there will be two in one bed and one will be taken; two working in a field, and one taken and the other left.

24. "In those days, after the tribulation, the sun and the moon will go dark. The stars will fall from the sky, and the very powers of nature will be shaken.

25. "That is when they will see the Son of Man coming in the clouds with great power and glory, and all the nations of the earth will mourn their end.

26. "Then He will send forward His angels to gather His elect from all the places on earth and no one shall be missed.

27. "Now, learn a parable from the fig tree; when its branches bud and put forth leaves, you know that the summer is almost at hand. So, too, when you see these signs, know that the Son of Man is near, even right at the door.

28. "Truly I tell you, this generation shall not pass away until all these things take place.

29. "But even if heaven and earth should pass away, My words will not pass away.

30. "No one knows when the end will come. Not the angels of heaven, not even the Son, but only the Father knows the day and the hour.

31. "Be aware, and keep on the alert, for you do not know when the appointed time will occur. Do not let your hearts be overcome by dissipation, drunkenness, and the worries of life, or that day will come upon you suddenly like a trap.

32. "It is like a master who goes away and leaves his servants in charge, giving to each his individual tasks and telling the doorkeeper to watch and wait.

33. "Therefore, be on the alert, for you do not know when the master of the house will return, whether in the evening, at midnight, or when the rooster crows when the morning comes. You would not want to be found sleeping.

34. "What I say to you, I say to all, watch!"

35. Then Thomas asked, "Lord, tell us how our end will come."

36. And Jesus said to him, "Have you found the beginning, so that now you are looking for the end? Truly I tell you, the end will be where the beginning is.

37. "Blessed are those who came into being before coming into being. Blessed are those who stand at the beginning; for they will know the end and will not taste death.

38. "For there are five trees in paradise for you, and they do not change from summer to winter, and their leaves never fall. Whoever knows them will not taste death."

39. Then Bartholomew and Thaddeus asked Him, "Lord, we know that You are going away. Who then will be our leader?"

40. And Jesus said, "No matter where you are you must find the one for whose sake heaven and earth came into being."

41. Then He told His disciples this parable: "When the Son of God comes as a king in great glory, He will divide the people of the world; some will be on His right and some on His left.

42. "And He will say to those on His right, 'Come, you who are blessed of My Father; inherit the kingdom prepared for you from the foundation of the world.

43. 'For when I was hungry, you fed Me; when I was thirsty, you gave Me something to drink; when I was a stranger, you invited Me in; when I was naked, you clothed Me; when I was sick, you cared for Me; while I was in prison, you visited Me.'

44. "Then the righteous will answer Him and say, 'Lord, when did we see You hungry and feed You, or thirsty and give You something to drink, or a stranger and invited You in, or sick and cared for You, or naked and clothed You, or in prison and visited You?'

45. "Then the King will say to them, 'Truly I tell you, when you did it for the least of My brothers, you did it for Me.'

46. "Then He will say to those on His left, 'Depart from Me, you accursed ones, into the eternal fire which has been prepared for the devil and his angels.

47. 'I was hungry, and you gave Me nothing to eat; I was thirsty, and you gave Me nothing to drink; I was a stranger, and you did not invite Me in; I was naked, and you did not clothe Me; I was sick, and you did not care for Me; I was in prison, and you did not visit Me.'

48. "Then they, too, will answer and say, 'Lord, when did we see You hungry, or thirsty, or a stranger, or naked, or sick, or in prison and not take care of You?'

49. "And He will answer them, 'Truly, I tell you, to the extent that you did not do it for one of the least of these, you did not do it for Me.'

50. "They will go away into eternal punishment, but the righteous into eternal life."

CHAPTER 38

1. Later, in a crowd where His disciples and some religious leaders were gathered, Jesus began to teach them about Himself saying:

2. "He who sent Me is true, and the things which He tells Me I speak to the world.

3. "I am the light of the world; whoever follows Me will not walk in darkness, but will have the light of life.

4. "For I do nothing on My own initiative, but I speak the things My Father has taught Me. He has not left Me orphaned, for I always do the things that are pleasing to Him.

5. "So it is with you: When you lift up the Son of Man, then you will know that I am He, and I do nothing of My own initiative, but I speak only what the Father has taught Me."

6. Some of the Pharisees said, "You talk about Yourself; therefore, what You say about Yourself is not valid."

7. Jesus answered and said, "Even if I testify about Myself, My testimony is true, for I know where I came from and to where I am going; but you do not know where I came from, and you do not know where I am going.

8. "You judge according to your flesh, but I judge no one.

9. "When I judge, My judgment is valid, for I am not alone in it, but I and the Father who sent Me judge together.

10. "I am one who testifies about Myself, and the Father who sent Me testifies about Me, and Our opinion is sufficient in its rendering."

11. So they said to Him, "Where is Your Father?"

12. Jesus said, "You cannot see Me for what I am, so you can not see the Father. If you could see Me, then you could see the Father as well."

13. Then He said to them, "I am going away, and you will seek Me, but you will not find Me, and you will die in your sin, for where I am going you cannot come."

14. So the Jews were saying, "Is He going to kill Himself? What does He mean, 'Where I am going you cannot come?'"

15. Jesus answered, "You are from below, but I am from above. You are of this world, but I am not of this world.

16. "Therefore; I tell you truly, unless you believe in me, you will die in your sin."

17. Then Jesus said to those who believed in Him, "If you continue in My word, then you are truly My disciples, and you will know the truth, and the truth will set you free."

18. But they said to Him, "We have never been slaves to anyone. How then can You say we will be set free?"

19. Jesus said, "Truly I tell you, anyone who sins is a slave to sin. The slave does not remain in the house forever, but the Son remains forever. So, if the Son sets you free, you are free indeed."

20. Then He said to the Pharisees, "You seek to kill Me, because My word has no place in you.

21. "I speak about the things I have seen with My Father, and you do the things that you have heard from your father.

22. "If God were your Father, you would love Me; for I proceed forth from God. I have not even come by My own volition, but rather God has sent Me.

23. "Why do you not understand what I am saying? Is it because you cannot hear My words?

24. "You are of your father, the devil, and you want to do the desires of your father. He was a murderer from the beginning and does not stand in the truth, because there is no truth in him.

25. "Whenever he speaks, he lies. And when he speaks a lie, he is speaking from his own nature, for he is a liar and the father of lies.

26. "Therefore, because I speak the truth, you do not believe Me.

27. "He who is of God hears the words of God; for this reason, you do not hear them, because you are not of God."

28. Then the Jews shouted, "You have a demon in You!"

29. But Jesus said, "I do not have a demon, but I honor My Father and you dishonor Me.

30. "Not that I seek to be honored by you, but the Father demands honor and judges accordingly.

31. "For that reason I tell you, if anyone keeps My words they will not taste death."

32. The Jews said, "Now we know you are demon possessed, for everyone dies. Abraham died, the prophets died. Are you greater than our father Abraham, who died? And the prophets who died! Who do you claim to be? For you say, 'If anyone keeps Your word, they will not taste death.'"

33. Jesus said to them, "If I glorify Myself, My glory is nothing; rather it is My Father who glorifies Me, the same Father you call your God.

34. "But you have not come to know the Father, but I know Him; and if I said I did not know Him, I would be a liar like you are, but I do know Him and I keep His word.

35. "The prophets and saints rejoiced to see My day, and they finally saw it."

36. The Jews said, "You are not even fifty years old, and yet You say You have seen the saints and the prophets?"

37. Jesus said, "Truly I tell you, before they were, I am."

38. And at that the Jews were beside themselves and picked up stones to kill Jesus, but He walked past them, hidden, for it was not His time to die.

CHAPTER 39

1. Now there was a man named Lazarus from the village where Mary, and her sister lived. And Lazarus was Mary's brother.

2. And Lazarus became very sick, so the sisters sent word to Jesus to come saying, "Lord, behold, the one whom You love is sick."

3. But when Jesus heard this, He said, "This sickness will not end in death, but it will end in the glory of God, so that the Son of God may be glorified by it."

4. Jesus loved Mary, and Martha (her sister), and Lazarus also; so, when He heard that Lazarus was sick, He stayed two more days in the place where He was.

5. Then after that time, He said to the disciples who were with Him, "Come, and let us go to Mary's house."

6. But John said to Him, "Teacher, it is in that same village that the religious leaders sought to kill You, and now You want to go back there?"

7. Jesus said to John, "Are there not twelve hours in a day? If anyone walks by day, they do not trip up, because they can see the light of this world.

8. "But if anyone walks by night, they stumble, because the light is not in them.

9. "Our friend Lazarus has fallen asleep; but I will go, so that I may awaken him out of his sleep."

10. And Thaddeus said, "Lord, if he is asleep then he will surely recover—we need not go there."

11. So Jesus said to them plainly, "Lazarus is dead, and I am glad for your sake that I was not there so that you may believe, but let us go to him now."

12. Then Thomas said to his fellow disciples, "Let us go with Him also that we may die with Him!"

13. When Jesus arrived, He found that Lazarus had already been entombed for four days.

14. Many of the people from Jerusalem had come to Martha and Mary to console them. And when Martha heard that Jesus was coming, she went to meet Him, but Mary stayed at their house.

15. Martha said to Jesus, "Lord, if You had been here my brother would not have died. But even now I know that whatever You ask of God, God will give it to You."

16. Jesus said to her, "Your brother will rise again."

17. Martha said, "I know that he will rise again on the last day at the resurrection of the dead."

18. Jesus said to her, "I am the resurrection and the life; anyone who believes in me, though they were dead, yet shall they live. And everyone who lives and believes in Me will never die. Do you believe this, Martha?"

19. She said to Him, "Yes, Lord; I believe that You are the Christ, the begotten One of God who has come into the world."

20. When Martha had said this, she went and called Mary, saying secretly, "The Teacher is here and is calling for you."

21. And when Mary heard this, she got up straightaway and went to Him.

22. Then the people from the Holy City who were with her and consoling her, when they saw that Mary left out quickly, they followed her, believing that she was going to Lazarus' tomb to weep.

23. But Mary came to Jesus and when she saw Him, she fell to His feet and wept, saying, "Lord, if only You had been here, my brother would not have died."

24. And when Jesus saw her weeping, and the people who came with her were also weeping, He was deeply moved in His spirit and was troubled, and He said to them, "Where have you laid him?"

25. So, the people said to Him, "Come, we will show you," and He went with them to the tomb entrance, and there He wept. And the Jews said of Him, "See how He loved him!"

26. Yet some of them doubted and said among themselves, "Could not this man who could restore sight to the blind even keep His dear friend from dying?"

27. So Jesus came to the tomb, which was a cave with a large stone rolled in front of it, and He said, "Remove the stone."

28. But Martha said to Him, "Lord, by this time there will be a terrible odor, for he has been dead for four days."

29. Jesus replied to her, "Did I not say to you that if you believe, you would see the glory of God?"

30. Immediately, she ordered the stone be removed. Then Jesus raised His eyes and said, "Father I thank You that You have heard Me. I know that You always hear Me, but because of the people standing here I have thanked You aloud, so that they may believe that You have sent Me."

31. And when He had said these things, He shouted into the tomb, "Lazarus, come forth!"

32. Then the man who had died came out of his tomb still bound hand and foot with wrappings and his face was bound with wrappings, and Jesus ordered, "Unbind him, and let him go."

33. A few days later, at Mary and Martha's house, Jesus was having supper with His disciples and Lazarus.

34. Mary then took a pound of costly perfume and oil and anointed the feet of Jesus and wiped His feet with her hair; and the whole house was filled with the fragrance of the perfume.

35. But Judas, one of His disciples who was intending to betray Him, said, "Why was this perfume not sold and the money given to the poor?"

36. Jesus answered him saying, "Leave her alone, for she has saved this for My burial. The poor you will have with you always, but you will not always have Me.

37. "Truly I tell you, wherever the Gospel is preached in the whole world, what this woman has done will also be spoken of in memory of her."

38. Therefore, many of the people who came to Mary and saw what Jesus had done believed in Him.

39. But some went to the chief priests and Pharisees and told them the things that Jesus did, and they began to plot how they would kill Jesus and Lazarus on account that many of the people were flocking to Him.

CHAPTER 40

1. After this, He left to go to Jerusalem, and as they drew near they reached a village on the outskirts.

2. He sent two of His disciples, Peter and Andrew, ahead saying, "Go into the village and there as you enter, you will find an untamed donkey that no one has ever ridden tied to a post.

3. "Untie it, and bring it to Me, and if anyone asks you, 'Why are you untying it?' say to them, 'The Lord has need of it, and will return it straight away.'"

4. So, Peter and Andrew went away and found the donkey just as Jesus had told them they would. And as they were untying it, the owners of it said to them, "Why are you untying our donkey?"

5. And Peter said to them, "The Lord has need of it." So the owners gave their permission.

6. Then they brought it to Jesus and threw their coats on it for a saddle and put Jesus on it. And as He was traveling toward the village, many believers came to Him and spread their coats on the ground in front of Him, or cut palm leaves and laid those down before Him.

7. Many at that time began to praise Him for all the miracles they had seen, shouting: "Blessed is the king who comes in the name of God! Peace in heaven and glory in the highest!"

8. Now some of the Pharisees in the multitude heard this and said among themselves, "See how this is getting us nowhere; the whole world has gone after Him."

9. And they came up to Him and said, "Teacher, rebuke Your disciples. They should not honor You this way."

10. But Jesus answered them: "Truly I tell you, if they were to stop, the very stones on the ground would cry out!"

11. Now, when Jesus and His disciples approached Jerusalem, He saw the city and He wept over it saying, "If you, even you, had known on this day what would bring you peace— but now it is hidden from your eyes.

12. "The days will come upon you when your enemies will build an embankment against you and encircle you and hem you in on every side.

13. "They will level you to the ground, you and your children within your walls. They will not leave one stone upon another. For you did not recognize the time of your visitation."

14. And as they continued, they came near a fig tree, and Jesus was hungry. When He saw that the fig tree had no fruit (for the season for figs was not at hand), He said to the tree, "May no one ever eat your fruit again." And His disciples heard Him say this.

15. When they entered the city they went to the temple, and Jesus found many there who were buying and selling.

16. Therefore, He made a whip out of lengths of rope, and began driving the merchants out of the temple. He overturned their tables and spilled their money and coins about the floor, and would not allow anyone to carry merchandise inside the temple.

17. And He shouted at them saying, "My Father's house is a house of prayer. You have made it into a den of thieves!"

18. And many blind and lame came to Him in the temple that day, and He healed them.

19. And the people asked Him, "What sign do You give to show You have authority to do this?"

20. So Jesus answered them, "Destroy this temple, and in three days, I will raise it up."

21. But they said to Him, "It took forty years to build this temple, how will You raise it up in three days?"

22. But He was speaking to them about the temple of His body.

23. The religious leaders, therefore, began to seek how they could destroy Him, for they were afraid of Him, for the whole crowd was cheering Him.

24. And the religious leaders became indignant at the crowd that was praising Jesus for His actions, and that they were calling Him "God on Earth," and they said to Him, "Do You hear what these children are saying? Why do You not stop them?"

25. But Jesus said, "Do you not know that out of the mouths of infants and nursing babies, the Father has prepared praise for Himself?"

26. And Jesus sat down and began to teach in the temple, and the people hung on His every word.

27. Though many believed in Jesus after He disrupted the selling in the temple, He did not entrust Himself to them, for He knew what people were like in their heart, and He did not require their testimony about Him.

28. That evening He and His disciples left Jerusalem and slept in the outer gardens.

29. In the morning, as they were returning to the Holy City, they passed the fig tree that Jesus had cursed the previous day, and they found it shriveled to the root.

30. Seeing this, His disciples were amazed and asked, "How did the fig tree wither so quickly?"

31. And Jesus said to them, "Truly I tell you, if you have faith, and do not doubt, but rather believe in your heart that what you say is going to happen, you will not only do what was done to the fig tree, but again I tell you, if you say to a mountain, 'Be cast into the ocean,' it will be done as well.

32. "Have faith in God. And when you pray, believe that you have received what you ask for, and it will be granted to you.

CHAPTER 41

1. When Jesus returned to the temple, He began to teach, and the religious leaders came to Him and asked Him, "By what authority are You doing these things; who gave You this authority?"

2. Jesus said to them, "I will ask you one thing, and if you answer me, I will also tell you by what authority I do these things.

3. "The baptism of John, from what source was it? Was it from heaven or from man?"

4. And the religious leaders reasoned among themselves and said, "If we say John's baptism was from heaven, He will say to us, 'Then why did you not believe him?' But if we say it was from man, then the people will rise up and stone us for they all regard John the Baptist as a real prophet."

5. So they said to Jesus, "We do not know."

6. And Jesus said to them, "Neither will I tell you by what authority I do these things."

7. Then Jesus told a parable saying, "There was a landowner who planted a vineyard and put a wall around it, and dug a wine press in it, and built a tower, and then he rented it out to some workers and went on a long journey.

8. "When the time for the harvest approached, the landowner sent his servants to the workers to collect his share of the profits.

9. "But the workers took the servants and beat one, killed another, and stoned a third.

10. "Again, the landowner sent another group of servants, even more than the first, and they did the same to them.

11. "Then he sent his own son to them saying, 'Surely, they will respect my only child.'

12. "But when the workers saw the son, they said among themselves, 'This is the heir; let us kill him and steal his inheritance.'

13. "So they took the only child of the landowner and threw him out of the vineyard and killed him.

14. "Now, when the owner of the vineyard comes, what will he do to those workers"?

15. And they said to Jesus, "He will kill those workers and rent out the vineyard to those who will pay him his share in due season."

16. Then Jesus said to them, "Truly I tell you, the stone which the builders rejected has become the corner stone; this turn of events came about from God and it is a marvelous work.

17. "And the one who falls on this stone will be broken to pieces, but the one on whom it falls will be utterly crushed.

18. "Therefore, I say to you, the Kingdom of God will be taken from you and given to a people who will produce fruit from it."

19. When the chief priests heard this parable, they understood that He was speaking about them, but they did not seize Him then, for the people considered Him to be a prophet. So they left Him for the time and went away.

20. But they watched Him, and sent spies who pretended to be righteous in order that they might catch Him in a statement that would make Him guilty before Governor Pilate.

21. Some questioned Him, saying, "Teacher we know that You only speak the truth, and You are not swayed by anyone's judgment of You, but You are always listening to God. Therefore, is it lawful for us to pay taxes to the government or not?"

22. Jesus, perceiving their evil, said to them, "You hypocrites; why do you test Me? Show Me a coin. Whose likeness and inscription is on it?"

23. They said to Him, "It is Cesar and it bears a government seal."

24. So He said to them, "Then render unto Cesar what belongs to Cesar, and give to God what belongs to God."

25. And at that, they realized they could not catch Him in a lawless statement in the presence of the people. And being amazed at His answers they remained silent.

26. Then some Sadducees (who say there is no resurrection) came to Jesus to question Him, and they asked Him, "Teacher, if a man dies and his wife remarries, and then that man dies, and the wife remarries again, and then that man dies, and finally the wife, herself, dies; If there is a resurrection of the dead in heaven, whose wife will she be?"

27. Jesus said to them, "You do not understand the power of God. For the children of this age marry and are given in marriage, but those who are found worthy to enter the kingdom of heaven neither marry nor are they given in marriage, for they are like angels and are the Children of God.

28. "And as for the resurrection of the dead, the God is not the God of the dead, but of the living. You fail to recognize that and are greatly mistaken.

29. "But you who have studied without ceasing are lacking in the knowledge of your nature, and therefore are utterly lacking. For you are like those who love the fruit of a tree but hate the tree; or you love the tree but hate the fruit.

30. "And how miserable is a person that depends on a body, and how miserable is the soul that depends on these two."

31. Then a scribe tested Him by asking, "Which is the greatest commandment?"

32. And Jesus said to him, "You shall love the Lord, your God, with all your heart, all your soul, all your mind, and with all your strength. This is the greatest commandment.

33. "The second is like it: You shall love your neighbor as yourself.

34. "These two are the foundation of the law and the prophets."

CHAPTER 42

1. Then Jesus spoke to His disciples saying, "The scribes and the Pharisees sit on Moses' seat; so practice and observe whatever they tell you, but not what they do; for they do not practice what they preach.

2. "They tie heavy burdens on your back, but they themselves are unwilling to move their finger to carry them.

3. "They do all their deeds to be seen by men; for they make their phylacteries broad and their fringes long. And they love the place of honor at feasts and the best seats in the synagogues. They love the salutations in the market places, and being called rabbi by men.

4. "But you are not to be called rabbi, for you have one teacher, and you are all brethren. And call no man your father on earth, for you have one Father, who is in heaven. Neither be called masters, for you have one master, the Christ.

5. He who is greatest among you shall be your servant. For whoever exalts himself will be humbled, and whoever humbles himself will be exalted.

6. Then Jesus showed to His disciples the rich putting their gifts into the temple treasury. And He showed them a poor widow putting in two small copper coins.

7. And He said to them, "Truly I say to you, this poor widow has put in more than all of the rich people did.

8. "For they have given out of their surplus, but she has given all that she had to live on—even from her poverty."

9. Then Jesus said to the religious leaders, "Woe to you religious leaders, for you travel the world to make one convert, and when they become one, you make them twice as much a child of hell as yourselves!

10. "You clean the outside of the dish, but the inside is full of robbery and self-indulgence.

11. "You brood of vipers and serpents; how will you ever escape your sentence of hell?

12. "Truly, I tell you that the prostitutes, tax collectors, and all form of sinners will enter the kingdom of God before you."

13. Then when Jesus had finished teaching, He said to His disciples in private, "You know that in two days the Son of Man is to be handed over for crucifixion, but do not grieve.

14. "For truly I tell you, unless a grain of wheat falls to the ground and dies, it remains alone; but if it dies, it bears much more.

15. "If anyone is to serve Me, they must follow Me, and where I am, there they must also be.

16. "The one who loves their life in this world will lose it. Those who hate their life in this world will find eternal life."

17. But when the disciples heard this they were grieved and discussed among themselves how they could hide Jesus.

18. At the same time, the chief priests and the elders of the temple were gathered together in the court of the high priest, Caiaphas; and they were plotting how they might seize Jesus in secret and kill Him, but they were afraid of the people rioting if they did.

19. Then one of the disciples, Judas, came to them and said, "What will you pay me to betray Him to you?" And they offered thirty silver coins to him, and from then on, Judas began looking for a good moment to betray Jesus.

20. Therefore, Jesus no longer taught in the temple of Jerusalem. For though He had performed many signs, the people were falling away from Him on account of His hard teachings.

21. And even though some of the religious leaders agreed with Him and knew that He spoke the truth, they said nothing, fearing they would be put out of the temple—for they valued the opinions of men rather than the approval of God.

22. When Jesus was alone with Mary, Thomas, and John, He said to them, "What shall I say, 'Father, save Me from this hour?' But it was for this hour I came into being.

23. "Now judgment has come upon the world, and the ruler of this world is cast out, and if I be lifted up from the world, I will draw all man unto Me.

24. "I have come as Light into the world, so that everyone who believes in Me will not remain in darkness.

25. "For a little while longer, the Light is with you. Walk while you have the Light, so that darkness does not overtake you, for the one who walks in the dark does not know where they are going.

26. "Truly I tell you, while you have the Light, believe in the Light, so that you may become children of the Light.

27. "For the one who believes in Me does not believe in Me alone, but in Him who sent Me, and the one who sees Me, sees the one who sent Me.

28. "I am the Light that is over all things. I am all. From Me, all came forth, and to Me all is attained.

29. "Split a piece of wood, and I am there. Lift up a stone, and you will find Me there.

30. "If anyone hears My words and does not keep them, I do not judge that person, because I did not come into the world to judge the world, but to save the world.

31. "For the one who rejects My word has one who judges them—the very word I have given will judge them on the last day.

32. "For I do not speak from My own initiative, but rather the Father who sent Me has told Me what to say, and His words are eternal life. Therefore, when I speak, I speak only what the Father has told Me.

33. "So, whoever is near Me is near the fire, and whoever is far from Me, is far from the Father's kingdom."

CHAPTER 43

1. The next day, John and Peter came to Jesus and said, "Where shall we go to prepare for Your final meal with us?"

2. Jesus said, "Go into the Holy City, and a man will meet you carrying a pitcher of water, follow him, and wherever he enters, say to the owner of the house, 'The Teacher says, "Where is My guestroom in which I may eat My final meal with My disciples?"'"

3. "And he will show you a large upper room furnished and ready; prepare that room for us."

4. So, John and Peter did as Jesus said and found things just as He had said they would. Therefore, they prepared for their final meal with Him.

5. When the evening came, He arrived with the rest of the twelve, and as they were reclining at the table and eating, Jesus said, "Truly I tell you that one of you will betray Me—one of you who is eating with Me now."

6. At that, the disciples became grieved and said to Him one by one, "Surely, it is not I, Lord?"

7. And Jesus said, "He who has dipped his bread in the broth with Me is the one who will betray Me." But they had all dipped in the bowl with Christ, and no one knew whom He meant.

8. Then Jesus said, "The Son of Man must go out as it has been planned for Him, but woe to the one who betrays Him. It would be better for that one if they had never been born."

9. And Judas said to Jesus privately, "Surely it is not I, Teacher?" But Jesus knew that Satan had already put into the heart of Judas to betray Him. And Jesus said to him, "It is you. Therefore, what you must do, do quickly."

10. And immediately, Judas got up and left the room, and he went into the night. And no one knew what Jesus had said to him, but supposed He had sent him to get something for the supper.

11. Now, Jesus knowing that the Father had given all authority to Him, and that He had come forth from God and was going back to God, got up from the table and removed His dinner garments and put on old clothing.

12. Then He poured water into a basin and began to wash the disciples feet and dry them with a towel, as was the custom for the lowest of servants.

13. When He came to Peter, Peter said to Him, "Lord, are You going to wash my feet?"

14. Jesus said to him, "What I do, you do not understand now, but you will understand it hereafter."

15. Peter said to Him, "You will never wash my feet!" But Jesus said to him, "If I do not wash your feet, you have no part in Me."

16. Peter said, "Then wash not only my feet but my head and hands as well."

17. Jesus said to him, "He who has bathed needs only to wash his feet to be completely clean, and you are clean."

18. When He had washed their feet, and changed back into his dinner clothes, He said to them, "Do you know what I have done to you?

19. "You call Me Teacher and Lord, and you are right, because I am. If I then, the Lord and Teacher, washed your feet, you also must wash one another's feet. For I have given you the example to follow, and you should do as I did.

20. "Truly I tell you, a servant is not greater than his master, nor is the one who is sent greater than the one who sent him. If you know these things, then you are blessed if you do them.

21. "Truly I tell you, the one who receives the one I send receives Me, and the one who receives Me receives Him who sent Me."

22. While they were eating, Jesus took a loaf of bread, and after He had blessed it, He broke it into pieces and gave it to His disciples saying, "Take this and eat, for this is My body which is to be broken for you. Do this from now on in remembrance of Me."

23. And when He had passed the bread around, He took a glass of wine, and said to them, "Drink this, for this is My blood

which is shed for the forgiveness of sins, and behold a new covenant is given to you.

24. "Truly, I tell you, I have much desired to eat this final meal with you before I suffer. For I will not eat this bread or drink this wine again until the day I drink it with you in My Father's kingdom."

25. Then, together they sang a hymn, and afterward left the upper room and went out to the Mount of Olives.

CHAPTER 44

1. When they arrived, Jesus began to tell them His final words. He said, "Now is the Son of Man glorified and God is glorified in Him.

2. "And if the Father is glorified in His Son, the Father will glorify His Son straightaway.

3. "I am with you for only a short while longer, and though you will seek Me, you cannot go where I am going."

4. Then Peter said to Him, "Lord, I can follow You right now. I will go to prison and die for You!"

5. But Jesus said to him, "Peter, behold, Satan has demanded permission to sift you like wheat, but I have prayed to the Father that you will not fail, and when you have returned to Me, you will strengthen your brothers."

6. Then Peter said, "Even if everyone else falls away from You, I will never fall away. Even if I have to die with You, I will not deny You."

7. And all the others agreed with Peter.

8. Jesus said, "Dear Peter, before the rooster crows at dawn, you will have denied Me three times."

9. Then He said, "You will all fall away because of Me, tonight. For when the shepherd of the sheep is struck down, the flock is scattered.

10. "But when I have been raised from the dead, I will go ahead of you to where we first met, and you will find Me there."

11. But Peter kept insisting that he would die with Him, and all the others were saying the same thing.

12. In their last hours together, Jesus taught the eleven disciples who were with Him saying, "When I sent you out with no money belt or bag, and even without extra shoes, did you lack anything?"

13. They answered Him, "We lacked nothing."

14. Then He said to them, "Now, whoever has a money belt is to take it along. Likewise whatever they have, they are to take, and whoever has no sword, sell your coat and buy one.

15. "For I tell you, I will be numbered along with the criminals, for that which refers to Me has its fulfillment."

16. And the disciples said to Him, "Lord, look. Here are two swords." And He said to them, "It is enough."

17. Then Jesus said, "Do not let your hearts be troubled; you believe in God. Believe also in Me. For in My Father's house are many mansions; if it were not so, I would tell you. I am going there to prepare a place for you.

18. "And if I go and prepare that place, I will come again and take you unto Myself, so that you will be where I am. And you already know the way to where I am going."

19. Thomas said to Him, "Lord, we do not know where You are going; how could we ever know the way?"

20. Jesus said to him, "I am the way, and the truth, and the life. No one comes to the Father except through Me.

21. "If you know Me, you know My Father as well; so, from now on you do know Him and have seen Him."

22. Philip said to Him, "Lord, show us the Father, and it will be enough for us."

23. Jesus said to him, "Have I been with you for so long and yet you do not know Me, Philip?

24. "Do you not believe that I am in the Father, and the Father is in Me? The words I speak to you, I do not speak by My own initiative, but the Father living in Me does His work.

25. "He who has seen Me has seen the Father. How then can you say, 'Show us the Father?'

26. "Believe Me when I tell you that I am in the Father and the Father is in Me; or else believe on account of the miracles themselves.

27. "Know what is in front of your face, and what is hidden from you will be revealed.

28. "When you see the One who was not born of a woman, fall on your face and worship, for that One is your Father.

29. "Nor will I, Myself, leave you as orphans, but I will come to you. In a short while the world will no longer see Me, but you will see Me, and because I live, you too will live.

30. "In that day you will know that I am in My Father, with you in Me, and I in you.

31. "Truly I tell you, the one who believes in Me, the works that I do, they will do also; and greater works than these they will do, because I am returning to the Father.

32. "Then, whatever you will ask in My name, I will do so that the Father will be glorified in the Son. If you ask Me anything in My name, I will do it.

33. "Indeed, I will ask the Father, and He will send you a helper in My name, that He may be with you forever: that is the Spirit of Truth whom the world cannot receive, because it cannot see Him or know Him.

34. "The Spirit of Truth will teach you all things and will remind you of everything I have said to you. And you will know Him, because He will abide with you and will be in you."

35. Then Simon asked, "Lord, how is it that You are going to manifest Yourself to us and not to the world?"

36. And Jesus answered him saying, "The one who loves Me will keep My commandment, and that one will be loved by My Father, and I will love that one and disclose Myself to them.

37. "Behold, peace I leave with you, but the peace I give to you is not as the world gives it.

38. "Nevertheless, do not let your heart be troubled, and do not be afraid. These things I have spoken to you are so My joy may be in you, and that your joy may be made complete.

39. "I will give you what no eye has seen, what no ear has heard, what no hand has touched; behold, what has not entered into the human heart."

40. Then Jesus said, "If you loved Me you would rejoice at My going away, because I go to the Father, and the Father is greater than I.

41. "I will not be here to teach you much longer, for the ruler of the world is coming, and he has nothing in Me.

42. "Therefore, I have told you all this before it happens, so that when it does, you will believe.

CHAPTER 45

1. As they walked in the garden through the vineyard, Jesus explained, "I am the true vine, and My Father is the keeper of the vineyard. Every branch in Me that does not bear fruit, He takes away; and every branch that bears fruit, He prunes it that it may bear more fruit.

2. "Abide in Me; for no branch can bear fruit on its own, unless it abides in the vine, so neither can you bear fruit except you abide in Me.

3. "I am the vine and you are the branches. The one who abides in Me and I in them bears much fruit, but apart from Me, they can do nothing.

4. "Anyone not abiding in Me is thrown away as fallen branches that dry up, and they are gathered together in bundles and thrown into the fire to be burned.

5. "Any vine planted apart from My Father will not be strong. It will be uprooted and it will perish.

6. "Just as My Father has loved Me, I have loved you; therefore, abide in My love.

7. "If you keep my commandments, you will abide in My love, just as I have kept My Father's commandments and abide in His love.

8. "And that the world may know that I love the Father, I do exactly as the Father has commanded Me."

9. Then Bartholomew asked the Lord, "Teacher, what is Your commandment to us?"

10. And Jesus said, "This is My commandment, that you love one another, just as I have loved you. By this love you have, all people will know that you are My disciples.

11. "For no greater love is there than that one lays down their life for their friends. Therefore, you are My friends if you do what I have commanded you.

12. "If you love Me, you will keep this commandment.

13. "You did not choose Me, but rather I chose you, and I have ordained you to go and bear fruit and that your fruit will endure.

14. "And now I no longer call you servants; for the servant does not know their master's business. But instead I call you friends, for everything I have heard from My Father, I have made known to you."

15. Then James said, "But the world does not understand you."

16. Jesus said, "Know that if the world hates you, it hated Me first. If you were of the world, the world would love you as one of its own.

17. "But because you are not of the world, because I chose you out of the world, the world hates you.

18. "If they persecuted Me, they will persecute you. If they kept My word, they would keep yours also. But all these things they will do to you, because they do not know the one who sent Me.

19. "If I had not come into the world and spoken to them, they would be innocent, but now the world has no excuse for its sin.

20. "Had I not done among them the works that no one else has done, they would be without sin, but now they have seen what I have done and hated Me and My Father, and they have hated us without cause.

21. "For the one who hates Me hates My Father as well.

22. "Nevertheless, when the Spirit of Truth who proceeds from the Father comes to you, that Spirit will testify about Me, and you will testify also because you are with Me from the beginning.

23. "These things I have told you ahead of time, so that when their hour comes, you will remember that I told you about them, and it will keep you from stumbling.

24. "For the world will indeed make you outcasts from the temple, and there is an hour coming when those who kill you will believe they are offering a service to God.

25. "They will do these things because they have never known Me or God.

26. "But as for this world: Be passersby."

CHAPTER 46

1. Then Jesus said, "Now I am going to the one who sent Me, and no one asks Me where I am going.

2. "Instead, because I have said these things to you, sorrow has filled your heart.

3. "Truly I tell you, it is better for you that I return to the Father; for if I do not return to the Father, the Spirit of Truth will not come to you, but if I go, I will send Him to you.

4. "And when He comes, He will convict the world concerning their sin, their righteousness and their judgment.

5. "He will convict them regarding their sin, because they do not believe in Me. He will convict them concerning their righteousness, because I go to the Father, and you will no longer be able to see Me. And He will convict them concerning their judgment, because the ruler of this world has been condemned.

6. "So many things I have to say to you, but you cannot bear them now. But when the Spirit of Truth comes, He will guide you in all truth, for He will not speak by His own will, but whatever He hears from the Father, He will speak.

7. "And He will tell you about the things which are to come.

8. "He will glorify Me, because He will take from what I have and disclose it all to you. All the things the Father has are Mine; therefore, I can say that the Spirit of Truth will take what is Mine and reveal it to you.

9. "In a little while you will no longer see Me; but in a little while you will finally see Me, because I am going to the Father."

10. Then some of the disciples said to one another, "What is He saying to us? What does He mean that in a little while we will not see Him, and in a little while we will indeed see Him, because He is going to the Father? What can He mean?"

11. But Jesus knew that they were wishing to question Him, so He said to them, "Are you considering that I said, 'In a little while and you will not see Me, and then again, in a little while you will see me?

12. "Truly I tell you that you will weep and grieve, but the world will rejoice, but your grief will turn to joy.

13. "When a woman has labor, she is in pain, because her time has come; but when she delivers, she no longer remembers the pain, because the joy overtakes her when her child is born into the world.

14. "Therefore, you have grief now; but I will see you again, and you will rejoice in your heart, and no one will ever take that joy from you.

15. "Indeed, the Father, Himself, will be one with you, because you have loved Me and believed that I have come from the Father.

16. "And if two of you agree on earth about anything that they may ask, it shall be done for them by My Father Who is in heaven.

17. "For where two are gathered in My name, there I am in the midst of them.

18. "I have spoken these things to you in parables, but the time is coming when I will no longer speak to you in parables but will tell you everything directly from the Father.

19. "Behold, I came from the Father, and I have come into the world, but I am leaving the world again and returning to the Father."

20. Simon said to Him, "Now You are speaking plainly, and we can understand everything. Now we know that You know all things, and have no need for anyone to question You, and from this we know that You have come from God."

21. Jesus said to them, "But can you remain in me? If only it were so. Behold, the hour is coming, and is already here, for you to be scattered, each returning to their own home and leaving Me alone; but I am not alone, for the Father is always with Me.

22. "These things I have told you so that you may have peace in Me. For in the world you will have trouble, but have courage, for I have overcome the world."

CHAPTER 47

1. When Jesus had said these things, He lifted up His eyes to heaven and prayed, "Father, the hour has come; glorify Your Son so that the Son may glorify You.

2. "You gave Me authority over all people that I might give eternal life to those I choose.

3. "And eternal life is to know the only true God, and His Son, Jesus Christ, Whom You have sent.

4. "I glorified You on Earth by doing the work You sent Me to do. Now Father, glorify Me together with You in that same glory We shared together before the creation of the world.

5. "I have shown You to the ones You have given Me out of the world, and I will keep showing You to them; for they were Yours and You gave them to Me, and they have kept Your Word.

6. "And now they know that everything I have is given to Me from You; for the words which You gave Me I have given to them, and they have seen and truly believed that I came forth from You, and that You sent Me.

7. "I am no longer to be in the world, but they are in the world, and I ask You, Holy Father, that You would keep them in Your name, the name which You have given Me, that they may be one, even as we are one.

8. "I ask on their behalf; I do not ask on behalf of the world, but only on behalf of those whom You have given to Me; for they belong to You.

9. "While I was with them, I kept them in Your name which You gave to Me; and I protected them, and not one of them perished, except for the one doomed to destruction from the beginning.

10. "But now I come to You, Father; and I speak these things in the world, so that My joy may be made complete in them.

11. "I have given them Your Word, and the world hates them, because they are not of the world, even as I am not of the world.

12. "I ask You not to take them out of the world, but keep them from the evil one. They are not of the world any more than I am of the world; therefore, sanctify them in the truth, and it is Your Word that is truth.

13. "I do not ask on behalf of these disciples alone, but also for the ones who will believe in Me through the words they speak, that they may all be one, even as You are in Me, and I am in You, may they also be in us.

14. "For the glory You gave to Me, I have given to them, that they may be one—I in them, and You in Me, that they may be a perfect whole, and the world will know that You sent Me and loved them, even as You have loved Me.

15. "Father, let those whom you have given to Me be with Me where I am, so that they will share in My glory."

CHAPTER 48

1. Then Jesus came with them to a place in the garden where
    they could rest, and He said to His disciples, "Sit here
    while I go over there to pray."

2. He took with Him Peter, John, and James, and He became
    grieved and distressed, and said to them, "My soul is
    grieved to the point of death; remain with Me and keep
    watch."

3. And He went a little ahead of them and fell on His face and
    prayed saying, "Father, all things are possible for You, so if
    it is possible, let the hour of this cup pass from Me; yet not
    as I will, but as You will."

4. Then He came back to His disciples and found them sleep-
    ing, and said to Peter, "Could you not keep watch with Me
    for one hour? You must keep watch and pray that you will
    not enter into temptation, for the spirit is willing but the
    flesh is weak."

5. He went away a second time and prayed saying, "Father, if this cup cannot pass from Me unless I drink it, then let Your will be done."

6. Again, He came back to His disciples and found them all asleep, for they had grown tired and their eyes heavy. So, He left them again, and went away a third time and prayed in like manner.

7. When He returned to His disciples, He roused them and said, "Are you still asleep? Behold, the time has come; the Son of Man is betrayed into the hands of sinners.

8. "Arise, and let us go, for My betrayer is here."

9. While He was still speaking, Judas arrived, accompanied by a crowd and several temple guards sent with him by the Chief Priest and the elders of the temple.

10. And Judas had prearranged with them that his sign to them would be whomever he kissed on the cheek. That would be the one, and they should seize Him.

11. At once, Judas went to Jesus and said, "Teacher," and kissed Him on the cheek.

12. And Jesus said to Judas, "You betray the Son of Man with a kiss?" Then they laid hands on Jesus and took Him by force.

13. And Peter reached and drew out His sword and struck a servant of the Chief Priest, cutting off his ear.

14. But Jesus said to Peter, "Put your sword back into its place; All those who live by the sword will die by the sword; or do you not think I can ask My Father, and He would at once put twelve legions of angels at My command?

15. "The cup the Father has given Me, shall I not drink it?"

16. Then Jesus said to the crowd, "Have you come out with swords and clubs to arrest Me as you would arrest a thief? Every day I sat in the temple teaching, and no one seized Me. I spoke nothing in secret, but spoke openly to the world. Yet, behold, this hour and the power of darkness are yours."

17. Then they took Jesus, and all the disciples fled out of fear and left Him, even Thomas.

18. Those who had seized Jesus led Him away to Caiaphas, the Chief Priest, where all the Pharisees were gathered together.

19. Peter followed Him from a distance and went into the courtyard of the temple, and entered in and sat with the other people to see the outcome, and he was warming himself by their fire.

20. Now the Pharisees and Caiaphas were trying to find someone who would give false testimony about Jesus so they might have grounds to put Him to death. And while many gave testimony, it was not consistent nor was it convincing.

21. Finally, they found some people who testified that Jesus said, "I am able to destroy the temple of God that was made by hands and rebuild another in three days made without hands."

22. At this Caiaphas stood and said to Him, "Will You not answer these charges? How do You explain what these men are testifying against You?"

23. But Jesus kept His silence.

24. Then Caiaphas said to Him, "I implore You by the living God, Himself, that You tell us whether You are the Christ, the very Son of God!"

25. Jesus said to Him, "I am; and from now on, you will see the Son of Man sitting at the right hand of power and coming on the clouds of heaven."

26. At that, the Chief Priest tore open his robe and shouted, "He has blasphemed! What further testimony do we need? You all have now heard the blasphemy for yourselves. Now what do you think?"

27. The scribes and the Pharisees answered in unison, "He deserves death!"

28. Then they blindfolded Him, beat Him, slapped Him, and spit on His face from all directions and shouted at Him, "Prophesy to us, You Christ; who is it that hit You?"

CHAPTER 49

1. While Peter was out in the courtyard warming himself, a young woman, a servant of the Chief Priest, came to him, looked at him intently and said, "You are a follower of Jesus." But Peter denied before all those present, saying, "I do not know who you mean."

2. When he left the courtyard, another woman saw him and shouted, "This one follows Jesus!" But Peter swore, "I do not know who you are talking about."

3. Then a little later a bystander came up to Peter and said, "Your from the same place as Jesus, surely you are one of His followers." But Peter began cursing and swore again, "I never knew the man, ever!"

4. And immediately, a rooster crowed in the distance, for the dawn was coming.

5. Peter then remembered the words Jesus had said to him, "Before the rooster crows you will deny Me three times." And Peter began to grieve and sob bitterly, then he ran away and hid himself.

6. When the morning came, Judas, who had betrayed Christ to the religious leaders, saw that they intended to kill Jesus.

7. For this reason, he felt tremendous remorse and returned the betrayal money to the Chief Priest and religious leaders.

8. And Judas said to them, "I have betrayed an innocent man." But they said to him, "What do we care if you have sinned?"

9. Then Judas threw the silver coins into the Holy Temple and ran into the wilderness. There he took a rope and hung himself from a tree.

10. The Chief Priest took the silver and said, "We cannot put this money back into the treasury for it has been used as blood money."

11. So they took counsel, and bought with it the potter's field, to bury strangers in. Therefore that field has been called the Field of Blood.

12. Later, the religious leaders and Chief Priest took Jesus to the Roman governor Pilate and delivered Him to Pilate on the grounds that He was to overthrow the government.

13. And they said to Pilate, "We found this man misleading our nation and insisting that we not pay taxes to the government, and He calls Himself, Christ—the only begotten Son of God—and He claims to be the only king!"

14. Pilate questioned Him saying, "Are You a king?"

15. And Jesus said, "Are you asking this, because you have believed that I may be, or have others told you about Me?"

16. Pilate said, "I am not one of Jews, am I? Your own people have delivered You to me."

17. Jesus answered, "My kingdom is not of this world. If it were, My servants would have fought to prevent My capture."

18. Pilate said, "Then You are a king?

19. And Jesus replied, "You are correct in saying that I am a king, for this purpose I was born, and for this purpose I have come into the world—to testify to the truth.

20. "Everyone who is born of the truth hears My voice."

21. Pilate said to Him, "What is truth?"

22. Then the religious leaders protested loudly, charging Jesus with many other crimes.

23. And Pilate questioned Him, saying, "Do you not answer? Do you not see how much they are charging You with?" But Jesus gave no further response, and Pilate was amazed.

24. Pilate then said to the Chief Priest, "Take Him to King Herod to be tried, for this is his jurisdiction, and so they took Him to Herod.

25. But Herod, when he saw Jesus was very glad. He had wanted to see Him for a long time, and hoped that Jesus would perform some sign for him.

26. And Herod questioned Jesus at length, but Jesus said nothing, so Herod's guards beat Him and mocked Him, and then Herod sent Jesus back to Pilate for a trial.

27. From that day forward, following the condemnation of Jesus, Herod and Pilate became friends whereas before they had been enemies.

28. When Pilate saw Him, he said to the religious leaders, "I have examined this man, and I find no guilt in Him. Nor has Herod, for he has sent Him back to me, and behold, He has done nothing to deserve death.

29. "Therefore, I will only punish this man and release Him." For Pilate knew that the priests merely envied Jesus.

30. But the Pharisees and Chief Priest protested vehemently and shouted, "Crucify Him!"

31. At that time, Pilate was holding another prisoner who was guilty of insurrection, robbery and murder named, Barabbas. And in that season, it was the custom to release one prisoner based on the people's choice.

32. And while Pilate was sitting on the throne of judgment, he decided to let the people in general determine whom they wanted more, Jesus or Barabbas.

33. But the religious leaders had already incited the people to shout for Barabbas and to have Jesus put to death.

34. Then Pilate stepped out onto a balcony and asked the crowds below, "Who shall I release, Jesus or Barabbas?

35. And they all shouted for Barabbas. Pilate said, "Then what shall I do with Jesus?"

36. And they all shouted, "Crucify Him! Crucify Him!"

37. Pilate said to them, "But what evil has He done?" Yet the crowd only shouted louder.

CHAPTER 50

1. When Pilate saw that he was accomplishing nothing, but that a riot was about to ensue, he washed his hands in a bowl of water in view of the crowd and said, "I will be innocent of this blood."

2. And the Pharisees, the Chief Priest, and all the crowed shouted, "His blood shall be on us and our children!"

3. Then Pilate released Barabbas to them, and sentenced Jesus to the executioners to be scourged and crucified according to the will of the people.

4. And they took Him from the seat of judgment to the dungeon where the guards spat on Him and beat Him with a stick and slapped His face.

5. They dressed Him in a purple robe, and one of them twisted a crown of thorns and put it on His head. Another put a reed in His right hand.

6. All the while they mocked Him and knelt before Him saying, "Hail! king of the world!"

7. Then on Pilate's orders, He was brought back out for the crowd to view. He was wearing the purple robe and crown of thorns.

8. And Pilate said to the crowd, "I bring Him to you again to show you I have found no guilt in Him. Behold the man!"

9. But again the Jews cried out, "Crucify Him! For He has claimed to be the Son of God!"

10. For this reason, Pilate became even more concerned, and he took Jesus back to the seat of judgment and asked Him, "Where are You from?" But Jesus gave him no answer.

11. So Pilate shouted at Him, "You will not speak to me? Do You not realize I have the power to free You or to crucify You?"

12. Then Jesus answered and said, "You would have no power over Me were it not given to you from above. For this reason, the one who delivered Me to you has the greater sin."

13. After that, Pilate brought Jesus back out and said, "Behold, your king!"

14. But the Chief Priest cried out, "Crucify Him!" So, Pilate sent Him back to the dungeon.

15. Then after they mocked Him again, they took off the purple robe, and took the reed and beat Him on the head with it.

16. Then they put His own garments back on Him and lead Him out to a hill outside Jerusalem to be crucified. Along with Him were two criminals who were also being led out for crucifixion.

17. Along the way, they forced a passerby to bear His cross and to take it up the hill. And following Jesus was a large crowd, and in the crowd were women who were mourning and crying out in sorrow.

18. And Jesus said to them, "Daughters of the world, do not weep for Me. Weep for yourselves and for your children. Behold, the days are coming when they will say, blessed are those who never had children.

19. "The future will beg the mountains and hills to cover them, for if they do these things when the grass is green, what shall happen when it is dry?"

20. When He arrived at the top of the hill, they offered him wine to drink, mingled with gall, but when he tasted it, he would not drink it.

21. Then they nailed His hands and feet to the cross, raised the cross, and crucified Him.

22. And as He hung on the cross, the guards divided up His clothing, deciding who would take what by drawing lots. And the guards mocked Him, saying, "Why do You not save Yourself?"

23. And Jesus looked down upon the people who were crucifying Him and said to God, "Father forgive them, for they know not what they do."

24. As people passed by, they hurled insults at Him. They shook their heads laughing and saying, "So You were going to destroy the temple and build it again in three days, but You cannot even come down from Your cross."

25. As well, the Pharisees and Chief Priest were mocking Him saying, "He saved others, but He cannot save Himself?

26. "Let this Christ come down from the cross, then we will see and believe. If He is the Son of God, let God save Him if He delights in Him."

27. The two criminals were also crucified with Him, one on His right and one on His left. The one on His left hurled abuses at Him saying, "Why do You not save Yourself and us, too, if You are the Christ!"

28. But the one on His right rebuked the other saying, "Do you not fear God even in your hour of death? We deserve what we are getting, but this man has done nothing."

29. Then he said to Him, "Jesus, remember me when You come into Your kingdom."

30. And Jesus said to him, "Truly I tell you, this day you shall be with Me in paradise."

31. Three hours later, darkness fell across the land, and it stayed that way for three hours. And at the end of that darkness Jesus cried out in a loud voice, "My God, My God, why have You forsaken Me!"

32. Then Jesus said, "Father, it is finished. Into Your hands I commend My Spirit."

33. With that, He breathed His last breath, yielded up His Spirit; and Jesus died.

CHAPTER 51

1. After these things, a secret disciple of Jesus, named Joseph, received permission from Pilate to take Jesus' body down and bury Him in his own private tomb.

2. And Nicodemus, who had once come to Him in the night, brought a mixture of myrrh and aloes for His burial, and together they took Jesus and wrapped His body in fine linen and applied the spices and laid Him in Joseph's tomb.

3. Then Joseph and Nicodemus rolled a great stone in front of the tomb to seal the entrance, and Mary observed from a distance so that she might tell the others where Jesus had been laid to rest.

4. The next day, the Chief Priest and the Pharisees gathered with Pilate and said, "We remember that while He lived, He lied and said that He would rise again on the third day after His death.

5. "Therefore we ask that you have guards secure the tomb until the third day has passed, otherwise His disciples will surely steal the body and say to all that He has risen from the dead.

6. "Then this last deception will be worse than all His others."

7. So Pilate agreed and gave them a guard, and they went with the guard and secured the tomb and put a seal on the stone at the entrance.

8. Now on the first day of the week, as the sun was just rising, it being the third day after His death, Mary came to the tomb to anoint the body of the Lord.

9. And she worried that no one would help her roll away the large stone, but when she arrived, she saw that the stone had been removed from the entrance, and the guard was absent.

10. So she ran away to where Peter and Thomas were staying and said to them, "They have taken the Lord out of the tomb, and I do not know where they have taken Him!"

11. Then Peter, Thomas, and Mary ran back to the tomb, and when they entered it, they saw only the linen wrappings lying there. And the face cloth that covered His head was rolled up and lying by itself.

12. And the disciples were grieved for they did not understand what Jesus had told them, and how it was that He would rise again on the third day. So Peter and Thomas left to go to their separate homes.

13. But Mary remained outside the tomb weeping, and as she did, she looked back in the tomb and immediately saw two men in dazzling white garments sitting on the stone bed where Jesus was laid.

14. And the angels spoke to Mary saying, "Why are you weeping? And she said to them, "Because they have taken my Lord, and I do not know where they have laid Him."

15. Then they said to her, "Why do you seek the living among the dead? He is not here, but rather, He has risen from the dead. Behold, the place where they laid Him is empty. Do you not remember what He spoke to you while He was with you?

16. "Do you not remember that He told you the Son of Man must be delivered into the hands of sinners, and be crucified, and then rise again on the third day?"

17. When they had finished saying this, Mary turned around and Jesus was standing next to her, and the angels were gone, but she did not recognize Him. Then Jesus said to her, "Why are you weeping?"

18. And Mary, supposing it was the keeper of the grounds, said to Him, "Sir, if you have taken my Lord away, please tell me where you have laid Him, and I will take Him away."

19. But Jesus said to her, "Mary." And when He had spoken her name, she suddenly saw Him for who He was, and said, "Teacher!" Then she fell to His feet and hugged Him.

20. But He said to her, "Do not hold on to Me, for I have not yet ascended to the Father.

21. "But go to the others and say, 'I ascend to My Father, and your Father, and My God, and your God.'"

22. And Mary ran from that place and announced to all the disciples, "I have seen the Christ, and He is risen!"

23. But to many of the disciples, the words that Mary spoke were nonsense, and they did not believe her.

CHAPTER 52

1. On that very day, two men who had followed Jesus were walking to a village about seven miles outside Jerusalem.

2. While they were walking, they talked to one another about the things that had taken place while they were with Jesus.

3. And as they walked, Jesus approached them, and began to travel with them, but their eyes were prevented from recognizing who He was.

4. And He asked them, "Who is this man you are talking about?" And the two men stopped and began to grieve.

5. One of them, whose name was Cleopas, said, "Are you the only one visiting Jerusalem who does not know what has taken place these last few days?"

6. And Jesus said, "What things?"

7. And they said to Him, "The things about Jesus, who was a prophet and did mighty works and was favored by God.

8. "The Chief Priest and Pharisees betrayed Him to Pilate, and He was crucified. And all the while we were hoping that He was the one who would finally free us. It has been three days since His death.

9. "One of our company, Mary, said she went to His tomb and had a vision of an angel who said He was alive, and so we went to look for ourselves some time after, but all we found was an empty tomb."

10. And Jesus said to them, "You foolish men. How slow you are to believe all the things that the Christ has shown you.

11. "Was it not necessary for Christ to suffer these things to enter His glory?"

12. And beginning with Moses and all the prophets, he interpreted for them all the scriptures concerning himself, but still He did not reveal Himself.

13. And as they approached the village where they were going, He continued as though He were traveling farther. But they urged Him saying, "Why not stay with us for the evening? There is almost no daylight left."

14. So, Jesus went with them and stayed where they were at, and when He had reclined at the table with them, He took the bread and blessed it, and after breaking it, He gave it to them.

15. Then their eyes were opened, and they recognized Him; and then He vanished from their sight.

16. And they said to one another, "Were we not burning in our hearts as He walked with us and told us everything about the scriptures!"

17. And they got up that very hour and returned to Jerusalem, and finding the eleven they reported, "The Lord has truly risen, and He has appeared to us!"

18. Then as they were all gathered in one room, and the door was shut, Christ appeared in their midst saying, "Peace be with you."

19. And He showed them the holes in His hands and feet, and Thomas said, "Lord, it is You!"

20. And Jesus said, "Thomas, you believe because you have seen Me; but blessed are those who will believe without seeing."

21. Then Philip asked, "Lord, why can I not see the Father?"

22. Jesus answered saying, "When you see your likeness in a mirror you are satisfied, but when you see the image of yourself that came into being before you and that neither dies nor becomes visible, how will you bear that?

23. The Father is disclosed, but His image is hidden in His own light. Let the one who has ears to hear, hear this."

24. Then Andrew asked, "Lord will we miss the kingdom of God when it comes?"

25. And Jesus said, "The Father's kingdom is like a woman who was carrying a full jar of meal. While she was walking home along a distant road, a hole broke in the jar, and the meal spilled out behind her along the road.

26. "She did not notice, but when she reached her house, she put down the jar and discovered it was empty. Therefore always watch, and never sleep."

27. Matthew said, "Now You are like the ancient prophets that have come to Israel in the past.

28. And Jesus said, "But you have disregarded the living one in your presence and have spoken only of the dead. Look to the living one so long as you live, otherwise you may die, and then try to see the living one, but you will not be able to."

29. After that, Christ gave to them His final teaching saying, "All authority is given to Me in heaven and on earth. I have come from what is whole.

30. "Go, therefore, and preach the Gospel to all creation, doing so in the name of the Father, and in the name of the Son, and in the name of the Holy Spirit."

31. Then Christ breathed on them all and said to them, "Receive the Holy Spirit." And they each received the Spirit of Truth as Christ breathed upon them.

CHAPTER 53

1. When He had spoken these things, He turned to Peter and said, "Peter, do you love Me?" And Peter said, "Yes, Lord, You know that I love You."

2. Jesus said to him, "Then care for My sheep."

3. And He asked again, "Peter, do you love Me?" And Peter said, "Yes, Lord, You know that I do."

4. And Jesus said "Then lead My sheep."

5. A third time, Jesus asked, "Peter, do you truly love Me?" And Peter was grieved, because He knew why the Lord was asking him a third time, and he said, "Lord, You know all things. You know that I love You."

6. Jesus said, "Then feed My sheep.

7. "For, when you were young, you dressed yourself and you went where you wanted to go, but when you are old, you will reach out your hand and others will dress you and lead you where you do not want to go. So, follow Me."

8. Then Peter turned and looked at John and said, "What about Him, Lord? Is it the same for Him?"

9. And Jesus said, "If I want him to remain until I return, what is that to you? You follow Me."

10. Christ performed many other signs. So many, that perhaps there are not enough books to contain them.

11. But these things have been written that you might see and believe in Jesus Christ by the power of the Holy Spirit, and that by believing in Him, you will inherit eternal life in His name.

The End

For more information about Veridicanism,
please go to our website at:

Veridican.net

www.ingramcontent.com/pod-product-compliance
Lightning Source LLC
LaVergne TN
LVHW051047080426
835508LV00019B/1750